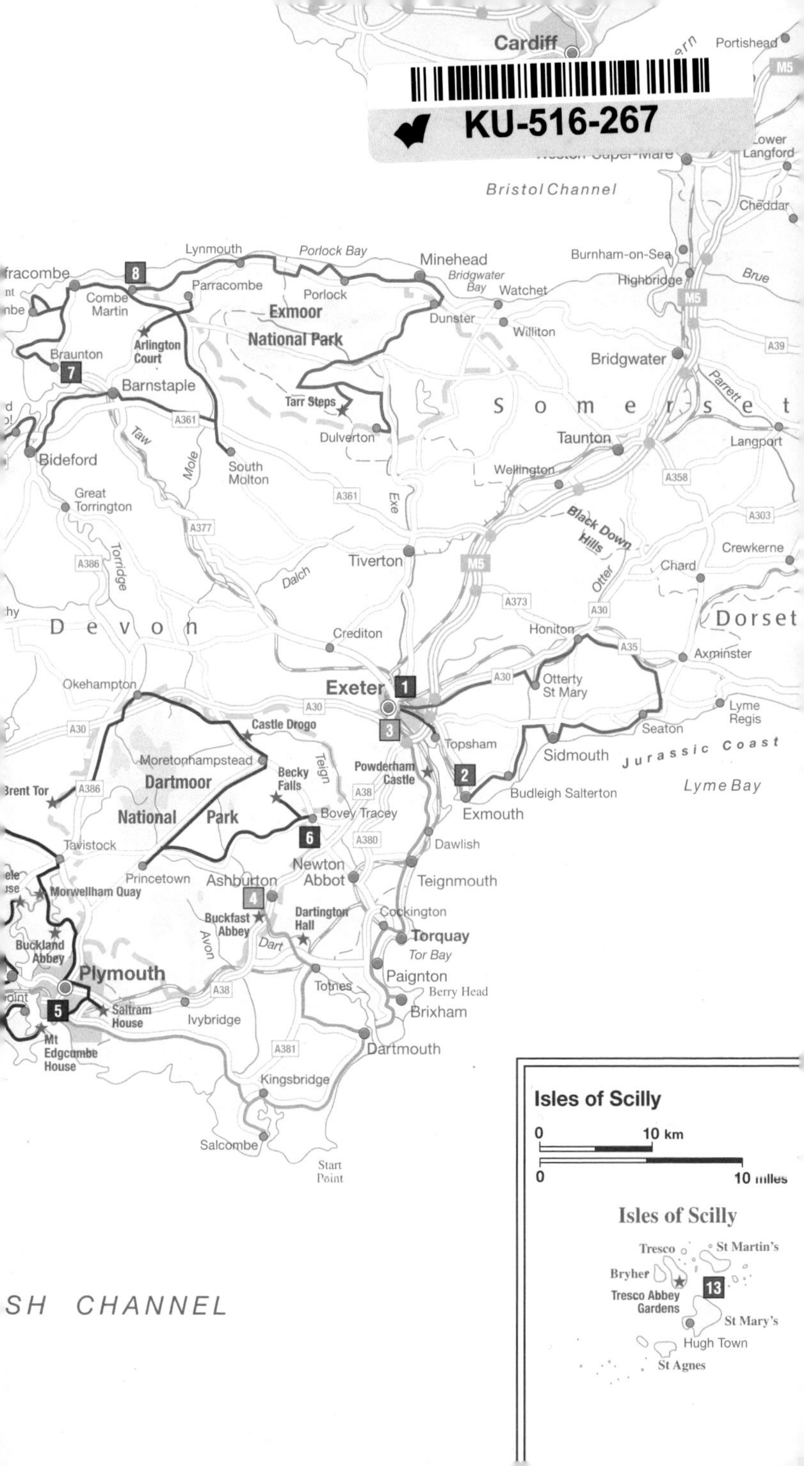
Cardiff
Portishead
M5
Lower Langford
Weston-super-Mare
Bristol Channel
Cheddar
Lynmouth
Porlock Bay
Minehead
Burnham-on-Sea
Bridgwater Bay
Watchet
Highbridge
Brue
8
Combe Martin
Parracombe
Porlock
Exmoor National Park
Dunster
Williton
Braunton
7
Arlington Court
Bridgwater
A39
Barnstaple
Parrett
A361
Tarr Steps
Somerset
Taw
Dulverton
Taunton
Langport
Bideford
Mole
South Molton
Wellington
A358
Great Torrington
A361
Exe
Black Down Hills
A303
A377
Crewkerne
A386
Torridge
Tiverton
M5
Chard
Dalch
Otter
A373
A30
Devon
Crediton
Honiton
Dorset
A35
Axminster
Okehampton
Exeter
1
A30
Ottery St Mary
A30
3
Lyme Regis
A30
Castle Drogo
Seaton
Topsham
Sidmouth
Jurassic Coast
Moretonhampstead
Teign
Powderham Castle
Becky Falls
2
Brent Tor
A386
Dartmoor National Park
A38
Budleigh Salterton
Lyme Bay
Exmouth
Bovey Tracey
6
A380
Tavistock
Dawlish
Princetown
Newton Abbot
Ashburton
Teignmouth
Morwellham Quay
4
Buckfast Abbey
Dartington Hall
Cockington
Torquay
Avon
Dart
Tor Bay
Buckland Abbey
Plymouth
Paignton
Totnes
Berry Head
5
Saltram House
A38
Ivybridge
Brixham
Mt Edgcumbe House
A381
Dartmouth
Kingsbridge
Salcombe
Start Point
SH CHANNEL
Isles of Scilly
0
10 km
0
10 miles
Isles of Scilly
Tresco
St Martin's
Bryher
Tresco Abbey Gardens
13
St Mary's
Hugh Town
St Agnes

[redacted]

Great Breaks

DEVON & CORNWALL

APA PUBLICATIONS
Part of the Langenscheidt Publishing Group

Contents

Travel Tips

Devon and Cornwall's Top 10

Many miles of wonderful coastal scenery, spectacular beaches, wild moorlands and great gardens make this the place to be outdoors. Indoors, you can see the painting and architecture the landscape has inspired.

▲ **Dartmoor** *(p.46)*. Devon's storehouse of ancient monuments, ponies and rare wildlife ranges from moorland to steep wooded valleys and secluded villages.

▲ **Lynmouth Cliff Railway** *(p.66)*. Designed by a student of Brunel, this marvel of Victorian engineering links Lynmouth with Lynton on the cliff above.

▲ **Dartmouth** *(p.32)*. This handsome Devon town is the pride of the Navy, where the Britannia Royal Naval College trains officers to rule the waves.

▶ **Tate St Ives** *(p.97)*. A sister of the London galleries, this is one of several great art centres in this Cornish fishing village that's been a magnet to artists.

▲ **Surfing** *(p.100)*. Surfers head for Fistral Bay near Newquay – the best surf beaches in Britain are here along Cornwall's north coast.

▲ **Torquay** *(p.24)*. Queen of the English Riviera, Torquay is an elegant resort with perfect examples of Edwardian wedding cake seaside architecture.

▲ **Tresco Gardens** *(p.110)*. Lush and vibrant, these exotic, tropical-looking gardens flourish year-round in the mild climate of the Scilly Isles.

▼ **Tintagel** *(p.104)*. Feel the power of myths at King Arthur's legendary Cornish castle, set on a wild headland.

▼ **Eden Project** *(p.78)*. Cornwall's most popular attraction, where vast domes provide the right climates for a dazzling variety of plants.

▼ **Exeter** *(p.14)*. Devon's county capital, Exeter has a majestic Cathedral, largely 14th-century and surrounded by superb lawns and medieval buildings.

Overview

A West Country Welcome

Warm, sometimes wet, always wonderful, this peninsula of high cliffs and moors, cream teas and thatched cottages has some of the most spectacular scenery in Britain.

Devon and Cornwall are holiday haunts par excellence. The beautiful, dramatic seascapes of high cliffs, delightful coves and broad, sandy beaches sweep along the extensive coastlines north and south. Fishing villages sit snug in coves, and river estuaries sigh with the ebb and flow of the gathering Atlantic tide. Small wonder artists have settled here.

If Cornwall inspires painters, Devon, the county that *Country Life* magazine declared the best in Britain in which to live, attracts writers. 'Deepest Devon' is an environmentally aware, agricultural land of thatched cottages and cream teas, run through with dancing river valleys and blind, winding lanes.

LEGEND AND REALITY

Covering 1,376 sq miles (3,563 sq km), Cornwall is a little over half the size of Devon. But this is the land of King Arthur, big on legend and fantasy, with pixies, smugglers, pirates, wreckers and saints, underpinned by haunting

relics of mysterious and ancient cultures. On misty moorland and along its rocky coast, prehistoric stone circles and burial chambers, cliff castles and hill forts punctuate the landscape, along with gaunt ruins from disused mines. Tin has been found and traded here since Phoenician times.

CLIMATE

Mild and sunny, warmed by the prevailing southwesterly wind – which also brings rain – the region is hospitable all year round. Flowers flourish everywhere; hedgerows are nature's gardens, while Devon violets and Cornish daffodils are among the first seasonal blooms in the shops each year. Spring comes early to the far west, and autumn lingers until late into the year.

When moisture-laden Atlantic winds hit the coast and swirl up to the exposed moors, they let go their load. Dartmoor, at 2,037ft (600m) the highest part of southern England, and Exmoor not far behind, each receives up to 90ins (230cm) of rain a year. Rivers

Above: characterful gallery near the village of Boscastle, in North Cornwall. **Below**: a clifftop wild-flower carpet.

Above: bronze statue honouring Cornish fishermen lost at sea, on the waterfront in Newlyn, Cornwall.

can swell and burst their banks with disastrous results.

But this is also the location of the English Riviera, in South Devon. The balmy, sheltered, palm-tree-lined resorts of Torbay hold the record for the warmest and sunniest days in Britain, with average September temperatures of 17.5°C (63.5°F).

The north coast is more inhospitable, and it shares with Cornwall a reputation for being a ships' graveyard. But that means good surfing too – some of Britain's best surf beaches are to be found here.

SEAGOING HERITAGE

The South Devon coast has a variety of safe anchorages, creeks and estuaries that in their day attracted traders and ship-builders. Crusades and *Mayflower* pilgrims set off from these southern shores. Devon was the birthplace of the Elizabethan buccaneers Francis Drake and Sir Walter Raleigh, and many Devonians have travelled widely in the merchant navy or in the armed forces, both of which have bases in the county, at Plymouth and Dartmouth.

Cornwall's maritime past is vital to its identity. Along 300 miles (482km) of varied coastline the spirit of 'free traders' is enshrined in the names of hidden coves, secret tunnels and caverns, and in the history of wonderful old inns. Cornwall's fishing activity fascinates the visitor at busy harbours such as Newlyn, Mevagissey and Looe, and the county's noble tradition of lifesaving is enshrined in lifeboat houses and coastguard lookouts.

ECONOMY AND TOURISM

Tourism is vital to the economies of these two counties, where natural resources are scant, and major commercial centres a long way away. Businesses tend to be small and self-employment is high.

Wage levels as a whole are among the UK's lowest. Traditional industries such as agriculture, forestry and fishing are low down on the list of money-making activities. The recession, along-

Above: beach babe in Looe, Cornwall's popular fishing village resort.

G Green and Gorgeous

After decades in the doldrums on the economic front, the two counties have been revitalised with a focus on sustainable development. There are revitalised docklands in both Exeter and Plymouth, wind farms, green hotels and houses coupled with a shift towards walking, cycling, bussing, boating, train travel, recycling and shopping in farmers' markets. Large-scale projects such as the Eden Project and the groundbreaking Wave Hub – a project to build the world's first large-scale wave energy farm off the north Cornish coast, completed in 2010 – have highlighted a collective desire to protect the region's resources. But while schemes like these dominate the news headlines, there are hundreds of accommodation providers, restaurateurs, food producers and community groups across the two counties working hard to keep Devon and Cornwall green and gorgeous.

Above: the revitalised quayside in Exeter, Devon.

with the recent poor summers of 2011 and 2012, have hit hard.

But Devon alone still numbers some 70,000 self-employed people, while receiving six million visitors annually. The county, along with neighbouring Cornwall, is turning to new enterprises, such as increasing the production of locally sourced food and employing green energy solutions. Initiatives are supported by the South West Tourism Alliance (www.swtourismalliance.org.uk).

Cornwall's remoteness meanwhile creates economic difficulties. The old Cornish industries have long been in decline; tin and copper mining are no longer viable, despite a conviction that Cornwall still holds vast mineral wealth in deep deposits. Of the old extractive industries, only a limited form of china clay and quarrying survive.

Cornwall's other great traditional industry, fishing, is struggling, and the people must rely on tourism. Almost five million visitors arrive annually, generating a quarter of the county's GDP.

WARM HOSPITALITY

Independence is at the heart of the local character. According to surveys, a West Country accent is one of the most desirable in Britain. Cornwall, once with its own language – at present undergoing a revival – retains a rebellious streak. But you will find the most friendly of hosts, and people who still have time to stop and chat. Don't be surprised if they call you 'my lover' or 'my handsome'. And if a Cornish person says *Dynargh,* they are only offering you a 'Welcome'.

Guide to Coloured Boxes

- E Eating
- F Fact
- G Green
- K Kids
- S Shopping
- V View

This guide is dotted with coloured boxes providing additional practical and cultural information to make the most of your visit. Here is a guide to the coding system.

Food and Drink

Shimmeringly fresh fish, lovingly matured farmhouse cheeses, crusty cottage loaves, local ales, award-winning wines, organic apple juice and traditional ice cream are just some of the delicious food and drink in Devon and Cornwall. Added to that is an haute cuisine revolution led by Padstow chef Rick Stein and incomer Jamie Oliver who have been making West Country eateries fashionable. But good food is to be found everywhere, as inns offer meals that go far beyond basic pub grub. Sustainability is key, and local means just that.

Above: Cornish pasties, devised as an all-in-one lunch for workers.

DELICIOUS DEVON

The food industry has a long tradition in Devon, dating back to the days when the ports were in their prime and flotillas needed provisioning. This tradition, combined with a scattered local population, has kept the supermarket culture at bay, with the result that Devon is now one of a decreasing number of regions where small town centres still have thriving markets, shops and traditional grocers.

Below: Devon's dairy farms ensure there are always great cream teas.

The huge Devonshire Cream Tea business is serviced by a large number of local dairies, which also produce a wide variety of local cheeses. This includes the Ticklemore Cheese dairy near Totnes, who specialise in blue cheese and supply local shops, including Country Cheeses in Tavistock. Another speciality is ice cream; try Salcome Dairy with an outlet in Kingsbridge Quay, Dunstaple Farm supplying the Exmoor area, and the Darmouth Ice Cream Company, with its shop, the Good Intent, located in the town.

The fishing industry is still important in the south of the county, so menus are strong on seafood. Local specialities to look out for are Brixham plaice, Dartmouth dressed crab and Salcombe smokies (smoked mackerel). There's a strong trade in home-made produce at most markets, with quality baking, as well as chutneys, mustards, marmalades and preserves of every kind on offer. One of the best locations is Barnstaple pannier market alongside the Butcher's Row line of shops.

Devonian drinking

Cider apples grow everywhere, and some rural pubs serve local scrumpy drawn from a barrel under the bar. Scrumpy can be an acquired taste, and packs a considerable punch. Grapes grow well in the south, with vineyards at Bickleigh (near Tiverton), Lower Eastcott (near Okehampton), and in a lovely location down to the shores of the Dart at Sharpham (Ashprington, near Totnes). Devon breweries include the Dartmoor Brewery and Exmoor Ales, while Tucker's Maltings, in Newton Abbot, is the only traditional malthouse (turning barley into malt for beer) in England open to the public.

CORNISH CUISINE

Cornwall has many traditional foods, but the Cornish pasty has become symbol as much as sustenance. Essentially an early form of 'fast food', the pasty evolved as an all-in-one lunch for miners, fishermen and farmers. A real Cornish pasty is a crescent-shaped pie of shortcrust pastry, crimped along one side. The traditional filling is chuck steak, chopped turnip, potatoes and onion, seasoned with salt and pepper.

It's a short step from pasties to pies, and here the Cornish cook is resourceful. Squab pie is filled, not with young pigeons as the name suggests, but with a mixture of lamb, apple, onions and sometimes prunes. Another favourite is Stargazy pie, made with mackerel.

The most traditional Cornish food is to be found in the seafood restaurants. You can expect salmon from the Tamar and the Camel on menus in those areas, and farmed trout almost everywhere. But best in the west of the county are lobster and crab, served in a variety of ways, together with oysters from Helford River and Newlyn crab chowder.

Cakes and ale

Figgy pudding is baked with suet, flour, eggs, sugar and raisins (not figs). Lighter alternatives are saffron buns, saffron cake and Cornish splits, cut in half and filled with clotted cream and jam. Cornish yarg cheese, wrapped in nettles, has recently been making a name for itself. And don't miss Metheglin (mead) and the local Spingo and Sharps beers.

For more culinary information, visit: www.slowfooddevon.org.uk, www.eatoutdevon.com, www.eatoutcornwall.com and www.tasteofthewest.co.uk.

Find our recommended restaurants at the end of each Tour. Below is a Price Guide to help you make your choice.

Eating Out Price Guide

Two-course meal for one person, including a glass of wine.

£££	over £30
££	£20–30
£	under £20

F Food Festivals

Celebrate all things foodie at these festivals. For more information, visit www.visitdevon.co.uk and www.visitcornwall.com.

April: Exeter Festival of Southwest England Food and Drink.
May: Torquay Food and Arts Festival.
June: Looe Festival of Food and Drink; Topsham Food Festival.
August: Newlyn Fish Festival.
September: Newquay Fish Festival; Cornwall Food and Drink Festival, Truro; Abbfest Food and Drink Festival, Newton Abbot.
October: Falmouth Oyster Festival; Dartmouth Festival of Food.

THE
POOPDECK RESTAURANT
Nº 15
mix—boox

FISH & CHIPS
TO LET
Y BELLE
XHAM

Devon Tour 1

Exeter and Topsham

Explore the highlights of this historic cathedral city and port on a full-day, 6-mile (9km) walking tour.

The county capital, **Exeter** lies on the River Exe in South Devon not far from the sea. It's a grand old market town (pop. 120,000) enlivened by one of Britain's oldest universities and an international airport.

The first recorded settlement (85–80BC) here was named Isca Dumnoniorum, after the local Dumnoniorum tribe. Around 100 years later the Romans transferred their West Country base from Seaton to Exeter, and the city began to take shape. In medieval times it prospered through farming and the wool trade, and it hallmarked its own silver until the early 19th century. But as ships grew larger, the river's facilities became inadequate, and it lost out to larger ports. Today it is seen as one of the top 10 places to do business in Britain.

Highlights

- Cathedral
- Underground Passages
- Royal Albert Memorial Museum
- Quayside
- Topsham

AROUND THE CATHEDRAL

The focal point for any visitor is the elegant **Cathedral Close**, screened from the modern city by a facade of buildings with a spread of diverse styles from several centuries.

At its centre stands the handsome **Cathedral Church of St Peter** ❶ (the Close; tel: 01392-285 983; www.exeter-cathedral.org.uk; Mon–Sat 10.30am–4.45pm, last entry 4.30pm; restrictions during services; free). Largely

Preceding Pages: Brixham harbour. **Left**: a statue of the Exeter-born Anglican theologian Richard Hooker (1554–1600) outside the cathedral.

14th century, its two towers date from 1050, when Bishop Leofric established a see here. He was enthroned on the site, with King Edward the Confessor in attendance. The nave is of Beer stone, started by Bishop Bronescombe (1257–80) and completed by Bishop Grandisson (1327–69).

The visitor entrance is located in the **West Front**, which is animated by figures of apostles and prophets, at ground level much weathered by devotional fingers. Inside, the most significant feature is the **fan vaulting**, which extends in a web of stone for 300ft (90m), the longest Gothic vault in the world.

The most eye-catching building in the close is the timber-framed 16th-century **Mol's Coffee House** ❷ (now a map shop) where Sir Francis Drake supposedly met his captains. Diagonally across, **The Royal Clarence**, founded in 1769, claims the title of Britain's first hotel – although it was actually just the first to be called hotel, thanks to its French owner. Outside the Clarence is where most of Exeter Council's free Red Guide tours meet (tel: 01392-265 203; www.exeter.gov.uk/guidedtours).

Tacked onto the corner next to Mol's is the small sandstone **St Martin's church** ❸ (founded 1065), which has a slightly crooked interior. Up St Martin's Lane to the left is the Ship Inn, also a Drake hangout.

MODERN CITY

St Martin's Lane emerges onto the largely pedestrianised High Street. The post-war rebuilding of Exeter is clearly visible here: to the northeast the street widens into a vista of stolid modern buildings, while to the southwest it

Fun on the Farm

For family fun head on down to Darts Farm in Topsham (tel: 01392-878 200; www.dartsfarm.co.uk). Pick up a map at the farm shop, then find your way through the maize maze. There are walks round the farm and an animal corner where you can meet the resident pigs, sheep, cows and chickens. Older kids can try fishing on the ponds for carp, bream and roach (charge) before picking their own fruit to take home.

Above: pick your own, go fishing or pat a pig at Darts Farm.

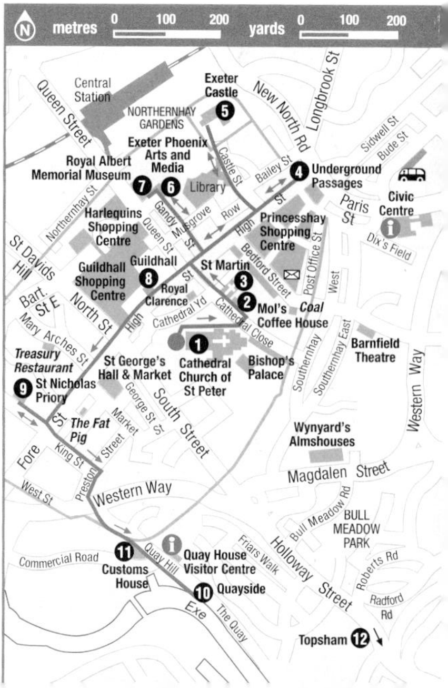

Above: the tidal estuary at Topsham is a rich habitat for waterfowl.

narrows into the uneven styles of old Exeter, with some medieval wood-timbered frontages.

Beneath the pavements of the modern area are the **Underground Passages** ❹ (Paris Street, entrance in arcaded Roman Gate Passage; tel: 01392-665 887; June–Sept Mon–Sat 9.30am–5pm, Sun 10.30am–4pm, May–Oct Tue–Fri 11.30am–5.30pm, Sat 9.30am–5.30pm, Sun 11.30am–4pm; charge), 14th-century tunnels that were carved out of the rock on the initiative of the clergy to help distribute water from a distant spring through the growing city. Although there is not much to see, the underground guided tours are entertaining and the experience unique, if cramped.

Up the hill behind the passages is **Exeter Castle** ❺ (also known as Rougemont Castle). Not a lot remains of the castle, and many of the buildings are now luxury apartments, but you can visit the courtyard, and the gardens are a delightful spot.

SHOPS, ART AND HISTORY

Retracing your steps to St Martin's Lane, diagonally to the north is the narrow **Gandy Street**, with murals and speciality shops. Topping a rise on the right is **Exeter Phoenix Arts and Media** ❻ (01392-667 080; www.exeterphoenix.org.uk) with a popular café-bar and a packed schedule of events.

Straight ahead you'll find the **Royal Albert Memorial Museum** ❼ (Queen Street; tel: 01392-665 858; www.rammuseum.org.uk; Tue–Sat 10am–5pm; free), reopened in December 2011 after a four-year redevelopment and featuring an eclectic mix from pre-history to fine art and world culture; in June 2012 the museum won the Art Fund's prestigious Museum of the Year prize. Back on the High Street further down, on the right-hand side heading south, is the tottery-looking

Above: inside the café-bar of Exeter Phoenix Arts and Media.

Tudor portico of the **Guildhall** ❽ (tel: 01392-665 500; times vary so check; free). It is the oldest functioning guildhall in the country: there has been a hall here from 1160, although the present building dates from the 14th century.

As it descends towards the river, High Street turns into Fore Street. Up narrow Mint Lane on the right is **St Nicholas Priory** ❾, the guest wing of a former priory, now brightly painted and furnished in the style of 1602, when it belonged to the Hurst family.

Back to Fore Street, descend the hill the other side of it and you will eventually reach the river Exe and the cobbled **Quayside** ❿ where history, antiques markets and nightlife live side by side. The visitor centre (tel: 01392-271 161; Easter–Oct daily 10am–5pm, Nov–Easter Sat–Sun 11am–4pm; free) gives a taste of what Exeter's port was like in its heyday. The old **Customs House** ⓫ (1681) is now occupied by a Fair Trade store, while the brick former warehouses hold shops and offices.

TOPSHAM

Continue walking or cycle 4 miles (6km) along the canal to **Topsham** ⓬, the estuary port at the mouth of the canal southeast of Exeter. During the height of the woollen trade in the 17th century, when the Exeter quayside began to prove inadequate, the merchants started to build grand houses on the shore at Topsham, creating an elegant waterside where passenger steamers used to dock until the railways came. The boatyards are still active.

Topsham's narrow-streeted charm is considerable. Antique shops, old inns, and restaurants line the main street, and along the Strand many of the houses are gable-ended, in imitation of Dutch style, a fashion introduced by Topsham merchants returning from Holland. Among them is the Shell House (1718), named after the lovely scallop shell in its doorway.

All the houses have fine views over the Exe estuary, which is a rich habitat for waterfowl.

E Eating Out

Exeter

Coal

18 Bedford Street, Princesshay Square; tel: 01392-420 070; www.coalgrilland-bar.co.uk; Mon–Sat 9am–11.30pm, Sun 9.30am–11pm.

With the cathedral as a backdrop, this stylish bar and grill specialises in food cooked over hot coals. £–££

The Fat Pig

2 John Street; tel: 01392-437 217; www.fatpig-exeter.co.uk; food served Mon–Thur 6–10pm, Fri–Sun noon–2-pm, 6–10pm.

The team at this convivial pub serve buzzy British dishes, smoke their own ham and bake their own bread. £

Treasury Restaurant

Mary Arches Street; tel: 01392-217 736; www.olaves.co.uk; daily lunch and dinner.

In the heart of the historic centre, this fine dining restaurant offers locally sourced dishes such as Fowey mussels and Brixham fish. ££

Topsham

The Fish Shed

Darts Farm Village; tel: 01392-878 206; www.dartsfarm.co.uk; Tue–Sat 11.30am–8.30pm, Sun 9am–3.30pm.

Select your fresh line-caught fish straight from the slab and a fisherman chef will grill it in olive oil or fry it in beer batter. £

La Petite Maison

35 Fore Street; tel: 01392-873 660; www.lapetitemaison.co.uk; Tue–Sat lunch (reservations only) and dinner.

Try the crab and king prawn bisque at this diminutive, award-winning modern British eatery by the estuary. ££–£££

Devon Tour 2

East Devon

This is farming country, interrupted by market towns and edged with elegant seaside resorts, which can all be taken in on a 50-mile (80km) full-day car tour.

Highlights

- Exmouth
- A La Ronde
- Otterton Mill
- Bicton Park
- Branscombe
- Beer Quarry Caves

This tour starts at **Exmouth** ❶, where the River Exe meets the sea. Its 2 miles (3km) of golden sand are the finest in East Devon. As one of the first seaside holiday spots, the Exmouth seafront has all the traditional attractions of a resort, as well as a big windsurfing centre.

Two miles (3km) out of Exmouth just off the Exeter road, **A La Ronde** ❷ (NT; Summer Lane, Exmouth; tel: 01395-265 514; Nov–mid-Dec Sat–Wed noon–4pm; Jan–mid-Feb Sat–Sun noon–4pm; mid-Mar–Nov 11am–5pm; charge) sits high on the hill with amazing views over the estuary. This eccentric 16-sided house was designed in 1795 by Jane Parminter, who, helped by her cousin Mary, decorated it with feathers and seashells, seaweed and sand, cut paper and marbled paint.

Leaving Exmouth, the B3178 winds around the hills before descending into **Budleigh Salterton**, a genteel place, with a long shingle beach framed in a red-cliff bay. At the east end are salt flats where the River Otter reaches the sea. Sir Walter Raleigh was born a couple of miles away at East Budleigh.

OTTERTON MILL

Two miles (3km) inland, towards Bicton, is a crossroads with a brick signpost that dates from 1743. Here in this lovely valley is **Otterton**, a village of attractive whitewashed cob houses with a stream beside the main street heading for the River Otter. In 1414 there were two woollen mills and a flour mill in the village, and boats could anchor by the bridge. **Otterton Mill** ❸ (tel: 01395-568 521; www.ottertonmill.com; daily 10am–5pm; free) is still functioning, in a complex with a restaurant, art gallery and museum.

A couple of miles further up the road are **Bicton Park** and **Bicton House** ❹ (www.bictongardens.co.uk; daily, Apr–Sept 10am–6pm, Oct–Mar 10am–4.30pm; charge). Henry Rolle's country house garden design of 1730 has been embellished with palm house, museum and a railway.

A right turn on the A3052 will bring you down into the crowded valley of **Sidmouth** ❺, the most attractive and best preserved of East Devon's resorts. Narrow lanes of tearooms and traditional shops back onto a grand seafront dominated by a parade of Regency houses with wrought-iron balconies.

Above: windsurfing at Exmouth.
Left: Branscombe's picturesque church.

Take the A3052 east for a couple of miles to the **Donkey Sanctuary** (daily 9am–dusk), a rest home for abused donkeys.

BRANSCOMBE AND BEER

From the sanctuary a lane descends into **Branscombe** ❻ (meaning branched combe or valley). There are corners of real beauty and character here; at the top end of the village is the 12th-century Norman church dedicated to the Welsh saint, Winifred. Grapes used to be grown in this sheltered valley for the monks of Sherborne Abbey.

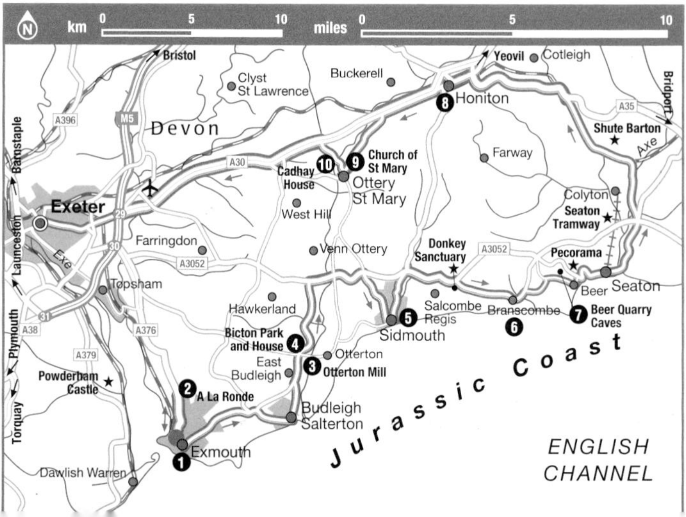

Branscombe was also known for its lace-makers, as was the next-door village of **Beer** (derived from 'beare', meaning wood), up over the hill. But besides smuggling and lace, Beer's fame comes from its limestone, used to build Exeter Cathedral and many other great churches and country houses of the region. Beer stone is unusual in that it is relatively soft and easy to quarry, but hardens on exposure to air. Part of the former underground workings are open to the public, on the Branscombe to Beer road, in **Beer Quarry Caves** ❼ (tel: 01297-680 282; www.beer-quarrycaves.co.uk; daily, Easter–Sept 10am–5pm, Oct 11am–4pm; charge). In these vaulted caverns, which supplied stone for 24 cathedrals, everything was done by hand. Many of the masons carved their names on the walls, and the pick marks made by the Romans are still visible.

Up the hill above Beer, **Pecorama** (www.pecorama.info; indoor exhibition all year, outdoor attractions Apr–May, Sept–Oct Mon–Fri & Sun 10am–5.30pm, Sat 10am–1pm; June–Aug daily 10am–5.30pm; charge) is an excellent diversion for children, with rides on small trains, entertainers, an outdoor play area and mini golf.

Above: the shingle and pebble beach at Branscombe.

The village of Beer itself clusters around a short main street which ends with a brief drop to the beach, where fishing boats are winched up and down the shingle. Beer's buccaneering past is still remembered in an annual regatta.

It is difficult to tell where Beer ends and **Seaton** begins, but the two places are very different. Seaton is a big, holiday-camp-based resort spread across the flat of the Axe valley, with a good beach and little of further interest other

Ⓖ The Jurassic Coast

Keen walkers can follow the South West Coast Path from Exmouth to Beer Head. This is part of the Jurassic Coast natural World Heritage Site, which continues to Studland Bay in Dorset, representing 185 million years of Earth history in 95 miles (153km) of coast. The East Devon rusty red section is the oldest and is home to Britain's richest mid-Triassic reptile sites. More info: www.jurassiccoast.com; www.nationaltrail.co.uk/southwestcoastpath.

Above: the Jurassic Coast has some of the richest fossil finds in the world.

Above: Shute Barton, a battlemented medieval manor house dating from the 14th century and one of the most important examples of its kind.

than the **Electric Tramway** (www.tram.co.uk), which runs up-valley in summer to the small town of Colyton.

On the side of the Shute road out of Colyton stands the imposing gateway of **Shute Barton** (started in 1380). Administered by the National Trust, the house is open to the public for tours four weekends a year.

HONITON

Continue on the A35 to the market town of **Honiton** ❽, administrative capital of East Devon. In the mid-19th century there were more than 4,000 makers of Honiton lace in the area, but the industry has since died. Presentation pieces are still made privately, and have been worn by all the recent royal babies. Examples are kept in All Hallows Museum and the Honiton Lace Shop *(see box, right)*, in the town centre.

A third of the way back to Exeter, south of the A30, is **Ottery St Mary**, a particularly attractive, largely 17th- and 18th-century town (Otrei in the Domesday Book) wedged into a small valley. The romantic poet Samuel Taylor Coleridge, son of the local vicar,

S Shops around Honiton

Many Honiton women still make lace as a hobby. Buy a sample or try out a lacemaking kit at the Honiton Lace Shop, The Barn, Elmfield Farm, Weston nr Honiton (by appointment only; www.honitonlace.com; tel: 01404-42416), or buy online. On Corrymoor farm in Stockland, Honiton (tel: 01404-861 245; www.corrymoor.com), the Whiteley family raises pedigree angora goats for mohair socks. The Brook Gallery, Fore Street, Budleigh Salterton (tel: 01395-443 003; www.brookgallery.co.uk) is the place to buy original prints and etchings.

Above: floral designs are typical of Honiton's bobbin lace.

was born here in 1772. Up a steep hill from the centre is **St Mary ❾**, a stunning replica of Exeter Cathedral, far more impressive from the inside than out. The church was founded by Bishop Grandisson, who completed Exeter Cathedral, and has a matching 14th-century astronomical clock.

A mile or so northwest of Ottery, and visible from the B3174, is **Cadhay ❿** (tel: 01404-813 511; www.cadhay.org.uk; May–Sept Fri 2–5.30pm; charge), a private house built around 1550 by solicitor John Haydon, probably using stone from local churches demolished by Henry VIII; every room has a different character. It is the residence of the William-Powletts, indirect descendants of John Haydon, one of whom may even be your guide. From Cadhay it is a mile (1.5km) to the A30, and thence back to Exeter.

Above: the beautiful fan vaulting in St Mary's church, Ottery St Mary, echoes that of Exeter Cathedral.

Eating Out

Exmouth

Brasserie 16

16 Douglas Avenue; tel: 01395-270 222; www.brasserie16.co.uk; daily breakfast, lunch and dinner.
The restaurant of the Devoncourt Hotel is set in fabulous subtropical gardens near Lyme Bay. At lunchtime on Wednesdays, Fridays and Sundays there is a renowned carvery. £–££

Les Saveurs

9 Tower Street; tel: 01395-269 459; www.lessaveurs.co.uk; Tue–Sat dinner only, opens 7pm, last orders 9pm.
For lovers of fresh seafood and fish, this is a must, and there are still choices for meat lovers, too. All are cooked with French flair, using seasonal, fresh Devon produce. ££–£££

Otterton

Otterton Mill

Otterton Mill; tel: 01395-56704; www.ottertonmill.com; daily 10am–5pm.
Dine on hunter's pie or a smoked fish platter either inside this historic mill building or outside on the sun terrace. This is also a good place for breakfast or a cream tea. £

Honiton

Café 102 Bar

102 High Street; tel: 01404-42739; www.cafe102.com; Mon–Sat breakfast, lunch and dinner, Sun 11am–3pm.
A little haven in the heart of Honiton, this bistro-style café-bar does hearty soups, nachos loaded with chilli, meaty mains sourced from local farms and delicious home-made desserts. There is also a garden at the back for those sunny days. £

Lakeview Manor

Dunkeswell; tel: 01404-891 109; www.lakeviewmanor.co.uk; daily lunch and dinner.
Wholesome English classics and a good-value Sunday carvery can be found at this lakeside cottage restaurant on the outskirts of Honiton. ££

Devon Tour 3

The English Riviera

This 49-mile (79km) half-day tour explores this coast, defined by sunny promenades, broad beaches and a refined gentility.

Highlights

- Powderham Castle
- Torquay Seafront
- Oddicombe Cliff Railway
- Kent's Cavern
- Dartmouth Steam Railway and River Boat Company
- Paignton Zoo

From Dawlish to the River Dart, Devon dedicates itself to tourism. Sheltered from the prevailing winds, this coast is a few degrees warmer all year round, making balmy resorts out of pretty fishing villages. The main attraction here is Torbay, not a town but an administrative umbrella for Torquay, Paignton and Brixham within 22 miles (35km) of the great sweep of Tor Bay.

Above: Powderham Castle, home of the 18th Earl of Devon.

POWDERHAM CASTLE

A short drive southeast from Exeter, in stunning parkland overlooking the estuary, is **Powderham Castle** ❶ (tel: 01636-890 243; www.powderham.co.uk; Apr–Oct daily 11am–4.30pm; charge), fiefdom of the Courtenay family, earls of Devon, and featured in the film *The Remains of the Day*. The building dates from 1390, the interior is grand and dramatic, and the guided tours are entertaining. Take the tractor trailer ride for a deer park safari.

Powderham's main entrance faced the estuary, until Isambard Kingdom Brunel bought the foreshore from the Courtenays and the Crown and built his railway *(see box p.24)*. Today the

Above: wedding day at Babbacombe Model Village – England in miniature.

line is a feature of this shore for many miles, such as at **Dawlish**. Dawlish first became popular towards the end of the 18th century, and both Charles Dickens and Jane Austen stayed here. Today it is a place of no great pretension, its character defined by the Long Lawn that runs down to the beach, the Bubbling Brook with black swans at its centre. Wilder bird life can be found on **Dawlish Warren**, the sandbar that covers most of the entrance to the Exe estuary. The sand-dune-backed Blue Flag beach is a popular picnic site.

Teignmouth, further down the A379, has a split personality. To the open sea it presents itself as a resort, with Grand Pier (1860s) and long beach, while the other side of the town lies along the Teign estuary and is still a working port. The coast road crosses the estuary via a former toll bridge to reach the pretty village of **Shaldon**, and then climbs the hill behind it, affording good views of the estuary.

TORBAY

You are now entering the Torbay area, although this approach is uninspiring and it is not until the **seafront** that **Torquay**'s ❷ full glory is revealed. The town is formed around inner and outer

Ⓕ The Riviera Line

One of the most scenic stretches of railway, the line from Exeter to Paignton sweeps along the sea wall and offers spectacular views of the Exe estuary and the red cliffs of the English channel coastline. Much of the surrounding countryside is a designated wildlife reserve. The line, built by Brunel in the 1840s, runs alongside the sea to Teignmouth before turning inland to Newton Abbot. From there it climbs and descends into Paignton.

Above: for 28 miles (45km), the railway sweeps along the coast.

harbours filled with leisure boats, a pier and spacious esplanade. The main shopping street, pedestrianised and with modern arcades, tunnels back up the valley. The harbourside and promenade has cafés, boat trips, theatres and the **Pavilion**, a lovely example of Edwardian wedding-cake seaside architecture, once a theatre and now filled with shops. Torquay emphasises its Mediterranean influences, and at night, with promenaders beneath illuminations and rustling palm trees, it could be Cannes or Monte Carlo. Almost.

Several attractions are concentrated around the former village of **Babbacombe**, on the north side of the Torquay promontory. The focus is the manicured lawns on top of an east-facing cliff overlooked by elegant small hotels, with Oddicombe beach way down below. The beach is reached by a zigzagging road, or by the **Oddicombe Cliff Railway** ❸ (tel: 01803-328 750; mid-Feb–Oct daily; also weekends Nov–Dec; charge), an attraction in itself. A short walk inland from the cliffs is the **Babbacombe Model Village** ❹ (tel: 01803-315 315; www.babbacombemodelvillage.co.uk; daily 10am–dusk; charge), contemporary England in microcosm, with sound and movement, created with much care and humour – look for the Ann Teak furniture shop and Penny Sillin the chemist.

BYGONES AND KENT'S CAVERN

A short walk away, in Fore Street, is **Bygones** ❺ (www.bygones.co.uk; daily Mar–Oct 10am–6pm, Nov–Feb 10am–3pm; charge), an indoor fantasyland of sights, sounds and smells, with a Victorian shopping street, model railways and a rather odd World War I trench experience.

Travelling a couple of miles east along the same road, **Kent's Cavern** ❻ (www.kents-cavern.co.uk; daily 10am–

Above: the promenade at Torquay, the Riviera's main resort, can have a dazzling Mediterranean air.

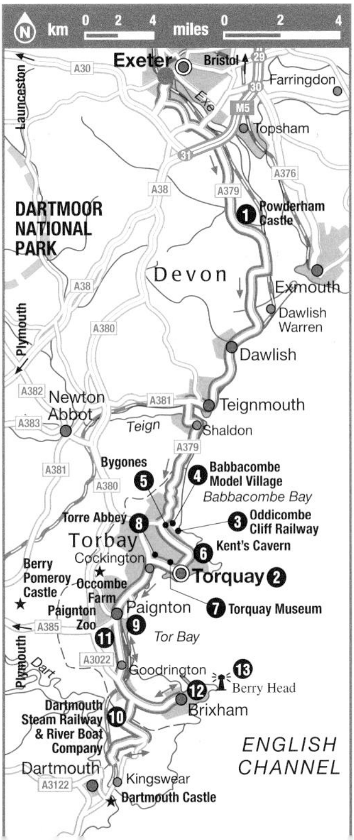

K Food and Farming

Occombe Farm (Paignton; tel: 01803-520 022; www.occombe.org.uk; Mon–Sat 9am–5.30pm, Sun 9.30am–4pm; free) is a working farm aimed at getting adults and kids involved in food and farming, as well as a great place to buy local food. There are farm tours, audio-guided nature trails and animals to visit, while year-round events include cookery courses with a special cookery club for children.

Above: a grunt of farmyard piglets.

4.30pm, ghost tours July–Aug Wed–Fri evenings; charge) is a network of limestone caves created two million years ago by underground rivers.

More than 80,000 archaeological artefacts have been found here, the best of them housed in **Torquay Museum** ❼ (www.torquaymuseum.org; Mon–Sat 10am–5pm, Sun mid-July–Sept 1.30–5pm; charge) on Babbacombe Road. Rated one of the best museums in Southwest England, the displays include artefacts from Kent's Cavern *(see p.25)*, a reconstruction of a Devon farmhouse and a gallery dedicated to one-time Torquay resident, thriller-writer Agatha Christie.

Above: grassy Berry Head.

On the other side of the harbour, away from the seafront, is **Torre Abbey** ❽ (www.torre-abbey.co.uk; closed for renovation until 2013/14 but can be viewed from the exterior). Torbay's art collection is housed in this 122-room former Abbey, once the largest of its kind in Britain, and visitors can see what it was like to live as a 12th-century Augustinian monk. Agatha Christie used to visit when the Abbey was a private home, and you can detect plants used for murderous poisons in the restored medieval garden.

Beyond Torre lies **Cockington**, a preserved rural village and country house in extensive grounds.

PAIGNTON

In the centre of Tor Bay, Torquay blends seamlessly into tacky **Paignton** ❾. Abundant with arcades and fast-food outlets, it does good business serving as it does two of the region's best stretches of sand, one off the promenade in front of the town centre, the other at Goodrington, a little further on.

Goodrington can be reached via the **Dartmouth Steam Railway and River Boat Company** ❿ (tel: 01803-555 872; www.dartmouthrailriver.co.uk; Apr–Oct; charge), which sets off from Paignton and chugs through attractive coastal scenery to its terminus at Kingswear *(see p.33)*, on the Dart estuary, where boat tours are available.

Up the valley behind Goodrington is **Paignton Zoo** ⓫ (www.paigntonzoo.org.uk; summer daily 10am–6pm, winter closing times vary so check on the website; charge), well landscaped

Above: the replica *Golden Hind*.

and innovative, and home to more than 50 endangered species. Micro-environments re-created here include Devon woodland, savannah and desert.

Beyond Paignton, the bay becomes less populated, and the road winds through countryside before descending to the small resort of **Brixham ⓬**, where tourism sits alongside a flourishing fishing fleet. The **harbour area** of Brixham has real character, both as a working and leisure port with extensive marina and, in the early morning, a highly active fish market (closed to the public). Moored in the inner harbour is a fine replica of the ***Golden Hind*** (www.goldenhind.co.uk; daily 10am–4pm; charge), the ship that took Francis Drake around the world in 1577–80.

The coast road leads up to the last headland in Tor Bay. Grassy **Berry Head ⓭**, now a country park, boasts the ruins of two forts built in 1803 during the Napoleonic Wars. It's a breezy place where locals walk their dogs, its limestone cliffs home to guillemots – known here as Brixham penguins.

A short drive back and over the headland from here (the steam railway takes the most scenic route) is the town of **Kingswear**, and the more appealing town of **Dartmouth** opposite, a brief ferry ride away *(see p.32)*.

E Eating Out

Torquay

The Elephant Restaurant

3–4 Beacon Terrace; tel: 01803-200 044; www.elephantrestaurant.co.uk; Tue–Sat evenings only.

With a Michelin star and overlooking Torquay bay, this is fine dining at the highest level. The less formal brasserie serves lunch (Tue–Sat). £££

Inn at The Grosvenor

The Grosvenor Hotel; tel: 01803-294 373; www.grosvenorhoteltorquay.co.uk; daily lunch and dinner.

For a taste of Devonshire cuisine you can't go wrong with these pub dishes. Good kids' menu, too. £–££

Babbacombe

The Cary Arms

Babbacombe Beach; tel: 01803-327 110; www.caryarms.co.uk; daily lunch and dinner.

This gastropub is all about a crackling log fire, slow-cooked specials and the lure of a proper pint. Great views. £

Teignmouth

The Owl and the Pussycat

3 Teign Street; tel: 01626-775 321; www.theowlandthepussycat.co.uk; daily lunch and dinner.

This Modern European restaurant does delicious Creedy duck and wild sea bass. Animal welfare and traceable ingredients are key here. ££

Brixham

Breakwater Bistro

Berry Head Road; tel: 01803-856 738; www.thebreakwater.co.uk; daily lunch and dinner.

Divers, ramblers and beachgoers come for the dressed Brixham crab, paella and ribeye steak. £–££

Devon Tour 4

The South Hams

Down the winding lanes on this 71-mile (115km) drive lie nuggets of interest and beauty including one of Devon's finest old towns, Totnes, and the historic port of Dartmouth.

The South Hams is a large, rural area between the Dart and the Tamar rivers, a flowing and verdant beard under the stony face of Dartmoor. The name derives from the old English 'hamme', meaning an enclosed and sheltered place. It has beaches and cliffs, forests and vineyards, deep river valleys and smugglers' coves.

This tour starts just beyond Newton Abbot, at imposing **Ashburton ❶**, north of the A38. Ashburton is a Dartmoor gateway, the largest in the National Park, and one of four strategically placed former stannary towns (with Plympton, Tavistock and Chagford) where tin from mines was weighed and appropriate duty paid. Its tall, well-preserved 17th- and 18th-century houses reflect the ensuing prosperity.

Highlights

- Buckfast Abbey
- Dartington Hall
- Totnes
- Dartmouth
- Salcombe

BUCKFASTLEIGH

Heading south, the Dart broadens considerably, brushing past hidden **Buckfastleigh ❷**. The town had a woollen industry (five mills still operating in 1890) but missed out on the tin wealth of Ashburton, and as a result is on a smaller scale, with small courtyards leading off its narrow main street. The textile industry is still here at the Buckfast Spinning Company at Lower Mills, which spins yarn for Axminster carpets, a mile (1.5km) upstream from the town. The mill merges almost seamlessly into the complex of buildings that surrounds **Buckfast Abbey** ❸ (www.buckfast.org.uk; Mon–Sat 9am–6pm, Sun noon–6pm; free), well preserved, and clearly laid out with something other than commercial interest in mind. The amazing story of Buckfast is well told in a small exhibition in the original guest hall. The Abbey church itself, Norman in style, has a certain freshness inside and nowhere more so than behind the choir in the Chapel of the Blessed Sacrament (added in 1966), with its glass Christ, arms outstretched.

There is still a small community of industrious monks at Buckfast. When they're not praying they're serving in the shops, bee-keeping or making tonic wine and coloured glass. Their produce shop uphill from the car park carries a revealing cross section of products from other self-supporting abbeys of Europe.

Left: Totnes Castle. **Above**: Norman tracery, Buckfast Abbey's west entrance.

Between the town and abbey is the **South Devon Railway** ❹ (tel: 0845-345 1420; www.southdevon-railway.co.uk; Apr–Oct; charge), a.k.a. the Primrose Line, a steam-hauled service that follows the River Dart to Totnes. There's a model railway, butterfly farm, rare breeds farm and otter sanctuary at Buckfastleigh station.

Above: Dartington Hall, which has the air of a university campus.

DARTINGTON

Travel on the train, however, and you miss the widely scattered **Dartington estate**, 2 miles (3km) north of Totnes. Most visited is the enterprise called **Shops at Dartington**, a group of 15 shops housed in and around a former cider-making building. Much of the high-quality merchandise reflects the Dartington emphasis on arts and crafts, with a particularly good selection of local foods.

This is the commercial side of the Dartington Trust, the creation of philanthropists Leonard and Dorothy Elmhirst, he English and she American, who had in mind a regeneration of rural life when they bought the Hall in 1925. His interest was in agriculture and hers arts and crafts, and the trust is now influential county-wide in many guises – the Plough Arts Centre, Dartington Crystal, Morwellham Quay and even in Dartmoor prison, where the trust provides further education.

For the nerve centre, turn off the A384 by Dartington church and follow it up a slow hill to the arts encampment over the brow, including the Barn Theatre and Cinema and research centres. Here is **Dartington Hall** ❺ (tel: 01803-847 070; www.dartingtonhall.com; free). Built in the 14th century, it has the atmosphere of an Oxbridge college, gathered around a cobbled quad and with a magnificent hammer-beamed Great Hall. Visitors can walk through to view the hall and the gardens beyond, where a variety of sculptures and a grassy-banked amphitheatre are set in mature woodland.

Above: retro details at South Devon Railway, Buckfastleigh.

Above: the Guildhall's sturdy pillars, once part of a Benedictine priory.

TOTNES

The Dart becomes navigable at **Totnes** ❻, a town of refinement frequently described as 'Elizabethan'. In fact its known history dates back to AD959, when 'Totta's Ness' (fort on a ness or ridge of ground) was established as a walled town by the kingdom of Wessex. It became a centre for the cloth trade, and in Henry VIII's time was the second-richest town in Devon after Exeter. The port has only recently stopped receiving cargo. As well as history, it has a strong arts culture and is fashionably alternative in an upmarket way, with its own eco project – a move towards a smaller, greener local economy; see www.transitiontowntotnes.org. for more information.

The face of Totnes has not changed for centuries, stretching up its one main street towards the castle, concealed from view by a tumble of crowding houses. At the river end of this street stands the memorial to William John Wills, a Totnesian who became the first man to cross Australia on foot (1861) and then foolishly tried to retrace his steps. Thereafter a variety of passages and frontages (Totnes' seasonal Elizabethan Museum is in a Tudor house at No. 70; charge) is interrupted by the arch of the East Gate across the road, marking the town wall.

A steep right directly under the arch leads up onto the ramparts and round to the **Guildhall** (Apr–Oct Mon–Fri 10.30am–4pm; charge), a lovely building behind a pillared portico that has its origins in a Benedictine priory of 1088, although the current structure is largely 16th century. The monthly council meeting still gathers around the table

S Shopping in Totnes

Quirky Totnes offers some unusual shops, but be warned – they are not cheap. For an ethical pair of handmade leather shoes which are sustainable and made to fit your feet in the style and colour of your choice, head to **Conker Shoe Company**, 28 High Street (www.conkershoes.com). Still on the High Street, at No. 94, you'll find the elite of the teddy bear world – Steiff, Hermans, Deans and Merrythought at **The Bear Shop** (www.bear-shop.oc.uk).

Above: small streets, small shops, but lots of interesting items to buy.

Above: the Boat Float is at the heart of the town of Dartmouth.

where Oliver Cromwell sat in 1646 after taking the town for the Parliamentarians, and the list of mayors dates back to 1359. The main street opens out into the Market Place, with the 17th-century granite-pillared **Butterwalk** on one side and rather unfortunate 1960s civic architecture opposite. This is the venue on summer Tuesdays (9am–3pm) for the small Elizabethan market, with traders in period dress.

Turn right at the end of the Butterwalk and within a hundred yards **Totnes Castle** ❼ (Apr–June and Sept daily 10am–5pm, July–Aug 10am–6pm, Oct 10am–4pm; Nov–March Sat–Sun

Below: haunted Berry Pomeroy Castle.

10am–4pm; charge) looms overhead. This is a plain but perfectly preserved Norman motte and bailey structure, whose simplicity adds to its power. One way the eye travels over crowded rooftops, and the other it climbs up onto Dartmoor.

A diversion out of Totnes just off the Paignton road (A385) is **Berry Pomeroy Castle**, a romantic ruin with pleasant woodland walks, but with a reputation as Devon's most haunted castle. The A381 from Totnes to Dartmouth is slow and winding, and there are plenty of potential diversions en route such as the Sharpham vineyard at **Ashprington**, with walks and tastings. From Ashprington a road heads southeast through Tuckenhay, down to the shore-side village of **Dittisham** (home to a few retired millionaires), with great views and a passenger ferry across the Dart. Known by the locals as "Ditsum", there are a couple of pubs, the Red Lion and the Ferry Boat Inn, in which to stop for refreshment.

DARTMOUTH

Nicely sheltered on the west bank at the end of the Dart estuary, the town

of **Dartmouth** ❽ is truly delightful. It faces the small town of Kingswear (vehicle and passenger ferries run year round, *see box p.34*). The waters are thick with boats in one of Britain's best anchorages. Dartmouth has a long maritime history, and a strong Navy presence on its shores and back up the hill above the town, where the **Britannia Royal Naval College** puts would-be officers, including many in the Royal Family, through their paces.

Dartmouth is focused on the **Boat Float** – an inner harbour full of dinghies – and the streets that run off it, crowded with historic buildings whose fine frontages are decorated with painted heads, coats of arms, and stained and leaded glass. A pleasant bandstand and garden where palm trees testify to the gentle climate occupy one side of the Float. The **Tourist Information Office** is in the same building as a small exhibition housing a working steam engine to commemorate Thomas Newcomen, inventor, who was born in Dartmouth in 1663.

On the promenade between the Float and the estuary stands the Station restaurant, Britain's only station without tracks: passengers would buy their train tickets here then hop on the ferry across to Kingswear, where the steam train from Paignton runs right down to the quay. The passenger ferry still runs.

Returning to quay level and heading away from the Float, it's a short walk to **Bayards Cove**, by the ferry landing. Bayards is less of a cove and more a well-preserved shore front, and has appeared as the backdrop to many films. At the end of the short prom is a

Ⓕ Dartmouth's Historic Centre

The granite-pillared 17th-century **Butterwalk** in Duke Street is well preserved and forms part of the Dartmouth Museum (6a The Butterwalk; tel: 01803-832 923; www.dartmouthmuseum.org; Apr–Oct Sun–Mon 1–4pm, Tue–Sat 10am–4pm, Nov–Mar noon–3pm; charge). Supposedly haunted, it showcases marine artefacts, shipping, shipbuilding and the Henley study, a child-friendly Victorian experience. Just up here, past the crossroads with pedestrianised Foss Street, is the solid old market, built around a cobbled square in 1828.

Above: the old Butterwalk has an original interior and a few ghosts.

Ⓥ Outer Froward Point

If you take one boat trip, be sure it's the one over to Kingswear – whose main attraction is its view, especially in the late afternoon. It is a 3-mile (5km) walk to Outer Froward Point from where there is a magical view of Dartmouth and the Dart estuary with its castles and cliffs. From the Royal Dart Hotel pub beside Kingswear railway station walk downhill then turn left up the Alma Steps. At the top turn right and follow the coastal path signs. More details at www.southwestcoastpath.com.

Above: the South West Coast Path is 630 miles (1,000km) long.

walk-in artillery fort built by Dartmouth Corporation in 1510, where high tide laps right up to the gunholes.

Bigger fortifications are a mile or so further south. **Dartmouth Castle** ❾ (tel: 01803-833 588; July–Aug daily 10am–6pm, Apr-June and Sept 10am–5pm, Oct–Nov 10am–4pm, Nov–Mar Sat–Sun 10am–4pm; charge), clamped to a shoulder of rock where the Dart meets the sea, is three elements: the original castle (1481), St Petrock's church (1642, although a church has been here since the 12th century) and a Victorian artillery fort.

The best way to see these castles and the Dart estuary is on a **boat trip**. Hidden creeks, imposing private houses, birdlife and sloping vineyards line its navigable 12 miles (19km) to Totnes. Boat is also the best way of reaching **Greenway** (NT; best to book, tel: 01803-842 382; Mar–Oct Wed–Sat 10.30am–5pm, also Tue mid-July to mid-Sept; charge). This lovely waterside property was the holiday home of Agatha Christie and her husband Max from 1938 to 1959.

Heading south from Dartmouth on the A379, the cliffs drop away first to **Blackpool Sands**, a delightful golden curve of a beach, fairly undeveloped despite its name, before running along the broad shingle at **Slapton Ley**, where an inland freshwater lake is thick with birds. US forces trained here for the Normandy landings of 1944, and locals had to leave their houses. The road dives inland here, but there is a fine cliff walk to **Start Point** via the remains of a village that has crumbled into the sea at Hallsands. From Torcross, continue on the A379 and head west.

Kingsbridge and Salcombe, respectively at the head and mouth of a 5-mile (8km) sea inlet, mirror Totnes and Dartmouth, although on a smaller scale. The steep main street at **Kingsbridge** ❿ is reminiscent of Totnes, as

Above: fishing on the curvy shingle beach of Blackpool Sands.

are its passages – find the aptly named Squeezebelly Lane just to the left of the Hermitage Inn. Its former town hall, incorporating the Reel Cinema, has a clock with three faces: the fourth side is blank, because it once faced the workhouse. At the top of the hill is a 16th-century granite-pillared Shambles, once a row of butchers' stalls but now a tearoom.

A leisurely drive south on the A381 will take you through lovely countryside. The sailing clippers at **Salcombe** ⓫ used to bring back the first fruit harvest from the Caribbean. Now this attractive fishing village, snug with lovely pubs, is a yachting centre, its narrow streets bursting at weekends. Sandy bays on the other side of the inlet are a short ferry ride from the town quay.

North from Salcombe, rejoin the A379. The coastline westwards from here is one of shipwrecks and secret smugglers' coves. Inland is a hidden rural landscape that repays exploration.

After the handsome 18th-century town of **Modbury**, it is a short drive to Plymouth *(see p.38)*.

Above: dinghies moored in picturesque Salcombe harbour.

E Eating Out

Dartington

Venus Café

The Shops at Dartington; tel: 01803-770 209; www.lovingthebeach.co.uk; daily 8.30am–5pm.

Award-winning, environmentally friendly café set in a stunning beachside location. Cream teas, all-day breakfasts and tasty salads are available. £

The White Hart Restaurant and Bar

Dartington Hall; tel: 01803-847 111; www.dartingtonhall.com; daily lunch and dinner.

Set in a medieval hall with Gothic chandeliers and ancient tapestries, this is an elegant place to enjoy single-suckled beef and grass-reared lamb. The cosy bar with an alfresco patio also has a children's menu. ££

Totnes

Waterside Bistro

The Waterside, The Plains; tel: 01803-864 069; www.watersidebistro.com; daily breakfast, lunch and dinner.

A great location beside the old Totnes Bridge with an outside seating area, this little gem does a great fish pie, breast of pheasant or wood-fired oven pizza. £–££

Dartmouth

The Angel Restaurant

2 South Embankment; tel: 01803-839 425; www.angeliquedartmouth.co.uk; Tue–Sun breakfast, lunch and dinner.

Chef Stephen Bulmer and his team produce stunning dishes using the best of local ingredients, with a particular emphasis on fish and seafood. Try the local fish of the day or, for meat-lovers, the griddled steak. ££–£££

Kingsbridge

The Sun Bay Restaurant

Inner Hope Cove; tel: 01548-561 371; www.sunbayhotel-hopecove.co.uk; daily lunch and dinner.

Overlooking the rugged coastline and sandy beaches of Hope Cove, this place specialises in line-caught fish from local fishermen, plus local delicacies such as mussels and crab. Children are welcome. ££

Literary Devon

Devon has inspired a host of literary greats and some classsic tales. Some authors were born here, others wanted to be sure their names were left here, carved in granite.

Soft light and outstanding landscapes have long provided fuel for the creative mind. They have also given Devon a literary heritage that's fun to follow as you tour the county.

HOMEGROWN TALENT

One of the most enduring classics of the county is RD Blackmore's highly romantic *Lorna Doone*, published in 1869, much filmed and never out of print. This 17th-century epic has given a new label to the upper East Lyn – the Doone Valley. Blackmore had the valley of Lank Combe in mind as the home of his outlaw family, the Doones (based on real Exmoor outlaws, the Gubbins), although the Malmsmead valley has since taken over the title.

Also a strong crowd-puller – even bringing the Japanese to Torquay – is Britain's most prolific author, Agatha Christie. Born in Torquay in 1890, Christie spent much of her lifetime in the area. She wrote two of her books while staying in the Art Deco hotel on Burgh Island. Her house, Greenway *(see p.34)*, on the banks of the Dart, is pointed out by pleasure-boat captains and there are exhibitions devoted to the writer in Torre Abbey and Torquay Museum.

Charles Kingsley, author of *The Water Babies*, was born in the Dartmoor village of Holne in 1819, although he is

more closely associated with the North Devon coast, particularly Clovelly, where his father was vicar, and Bideford, where the name *Westward Ho!* is named after one of his books.

Samuel Taylor Coleridge was born in 1772 in Ottery St Mary, where his father was rector, and although he spent most of his life elsewhere, he never lost his Devon accent. In later years the poet Robert Southey and Coleridge would carouse in the Ship Inn at Porlock Weir; and it was an unknown person from Porlock who so rudely interrupted the narrator in *Kubla Khan*.

John Gay, poet and author of the *Beggar's Opera*, was born in Barnstaple in 1685, and went to school in the charismatic St Anne's Chapel, where a small exhibition preserves some of the atmosphere of the time.

Above: fear stalks the Moors as Christopher Lee confronts the Hound of the Baskervilles. **Top Left**: Agatha Christie, whose home can be visited. **Bottom Left**: one of many screen adaptations of *Lorna Doone*.

INSPIRING DEVON

Many more giants of literature came here seeking inspiration. Arthur Conan Doyle visited Dartmoor, and used the name of his coachman-guide – Baskerville – in *The Hound of the Baskervilles*. Rudyard Kipling based *Stalky and Co* on his college life in Bideford.

Other writers and poets simply used Devon as a peaceful place for the creative process. Evelyn Waugh wrote *Brideshead Revisited* while staying in a hotel near Chagford, and John Galsworthy wrote *The Forsyte Saga* while living on a farm at Manaton, on the eastern side of Dartmoor.

In tourism terms, the biggest impact has been made by Henry Williamson, who came to settle in Georgeham, near Croyde. His are the most telling footprints on the landscape, thanks to the book and film of *Tarka the Otter*. Much of Mid Devon has been dubbed 'Tarka Country', with key points from the book along the Tarka Trail.

The poet laureate, Ted Hughes, who moved to North Tawton in 1961 and lived there till his death in 1998, loved and wrote about Devon's countryside. At his request, his ashes were scattered on Dartmoor. He also asked for his name to be carved in a slab of granite between the sources of the rivers Teign, Dart, Taw and East Okement. It's supposed to be there, but remains unrecorded as the site is on Duchy of Cornwall land – Hughes was a friend of Prince Charles.

Devon Tour 5

Plymouth and the Tamar Valley

Explore the naval city of Plymouth, then head north to the edge of wild Dartmoor. At Tavistock, cross the river Tamar to Cornwall on this full-day, 70-mile (112km) drive.

The largest city in Devon, and a major naval base, **Plymouth 1** (pop. 258,000) was so damaged in the last war it is mostly a new town. It was once three townships: Dock (now Devonport), Sutton and Stonehouse. The natural harbour, formed where the Tamar and Plym rivers debouch into the Sound, was already a significant port in the 14th century, controlling the English Channel. Numerous discoverers and pioneers set off on their epic voyages from here: Drake, Hawkins, Raleigh, Cook, the Pilgrim Fathers and half a million emigrants.

One night in 1941, 1,000 people were killed and 20,000 homes destroyed by German bombs. After the war, town planners scrapped what remained and started again. The result is a pedestrian shopping centre surrounded by traffic.

Although it is only a few miles from the downtown stores to the bleak uplands of Dartmoor, the contrast couldn't be greater.

Highlights

- Plymouth Hoe
- Buckland Abbey
- Launceston
- Morwellham Quay
- Antony House
- Mount Edgcumbe House

Left: the Barbican. **Above**: Smeaton's Tower, now high and dry on the Hoe, once stood on a rock far out to sea.

THE HOE

The setting for many of Plymouth's best dramas is the **Hoe** Ⓐ (old English for 'high place'), a broad, breezy, grassy shoulder between town and sea. It commands an extraordinary view of the Sound, laid out below like an amphi-theatre. This is where Sir Francis Drake was alleged to have been playing bowls when the Spanish Armada arrived in 1588.

In the far distance (14 miles/23km), the Eddystone lighthouse can be seen on a clear day. The current lighthouse is the fourth; the third, **Smeaton's Tower**, now stands on the Hoe, and is open to the public.

Several memorials line the Hoe leading to the formidable walls of the **Royal Citadel** Ⓑ. The fort was completed in 1671 by Charles II, shortly after Plymouth had taken the anti-royalist side in the Civil War, and its guns face both ways – over the city and the sea – although they have never been fired in anger. The Citadel is garrisoned by the Royal Artillery.

Well landscaped into the front brow of the Hoe is the **Dome**, a former innovative multi-media presentation of Plymouth's past and present, but with plans to re-open as a restaurant.

Plymouth's old Aquarium used to be here, but has since been reborn as the grand **National Marine Aquarium** Ⓒ (tel: 0844-893 7938; www.national-aquarium.co.uk; daily, Apr–Sept 10am–6pm, Oct–Mar 10am–5pm; charge) on the east side of Sutton Harbour. The emphasis is on education, but there's also a memorable shark tank.

Sutton Harbour is the watery part of the **Barbican** Ⓓ, a preserved corner of Plymouth as it used to be, from where many of Plymouth's historic voyages started out. The Barbican's shops, restaurants and galleries are attractively located in converted warehouses and merchants' houses, particularly along Southside Street. Towards the end of the street you'll find the **Plymouth gin distillery**, which welcomes visitors.

Plymouth is a city without a cathedral. **St Andrew's** Ⓔ, its principal

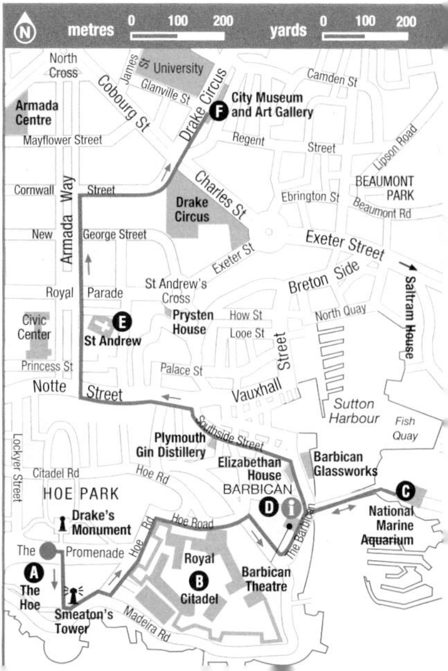

church, was largely rebuilt following the war, and is notable for striking glass windows by artist John Piper, as well as graffiti scratched into the masonry which is thought to celebrate Drake's voyage round the world.

The **City Museum and Art Gallery** F (Drake Circus; tel: 01752-304 774; Tue–Fri 10am–5.30pm, Sat 10am–5pm), behind the main shopping area, reflects local interests in a generalised collection, but also has some fine paintings by artists including Sir Joshua Reynolds and Stanhope Forbes.

DEVON WONDERS

Just off the A38 3 miles (5km) east of Plymouth stands the grand **Saltram House** 2 (NT; Apr–Oct Sat–Thur noon–4.30pm; charge), Devon's largest country house, in 470 acres (190 hectares) of grounds and 13 acres (5.3 hectares) of gardens. It has a fine Robert Adam interior and most of its furnishings are original. The house served as the Dashwood family home in the film of *Sense and Sensibility*.

Some 8 miles (13km) north of Plymouth, just off the A386 en route to Tavistock, are two West Devon highlights. **Buckland Abbey** 3 (NT; Apr–Oct daily 10.30am–5.30pm, winter check for weekend times; charge) belonged to the Cistercian order and dates from 1278. Dissolved under Henry VIII, it became a wonderful Elizabethan mansion, and home of Drake, who was born in nearby Tavistock. He bought the house in 1580 from his rival Sir Richard Grenville for £3,400.

Four miles (6km) north is **Morwellham Quay** 4 (tel: 01822-832 766; www.morwellham-quay.co.uk; daily 10am–5pm, winter 4pm; charge), the highest navigable point on the Tamar. Morwellham is a superbly preserved and presented snapshot of how in-

F The River Tamar

Nothing has done more to keep Cornwall Cornish than the River Tamar. From its springs at Woolley Barrows, just a few miles from the north Cornish coast, down to Plymouth Sound, it proved an effective barrier against the Romans and the Anglo Saxons, and provided broad waters and landing places for the ships that took away the produce of Cornish mines (copper and tin) and its quarries (granite and slate).

Below: Saltram House has year-round events including jazz picnics and theatre.

Above: beautifully preserved Morwellham Quay shows how the copper was transported on the Tamar.

dustry and thus transport ebbed and flowed in the region in Victorian times. It is set in a lovely valley, and animated by staff in period costume.

Morwellham existed as a port for a thousand years before the discovery of huge copper deposits in the region demanded the provision of heavy transport – so much so that a canal was cut from Tavistock to the hills above Morwellham, from where an inclined railway ran down to the quay. Eventually the mines were exhausted and the railway arrived, killing off water transport. Morwellham disappeared under weeds until 1970, when it became a project of the Dartington Trust which lovingly restored and created its museums and trails.

TAVISTOCK

The pleasant old market town of **Tavistock** ❺ benefited enormously from the prosperity of local copper and tin mining. The landowning Russell family (dukes of Bedford) created the town as it looks today, particularly the main Bedford Square. Plunge through the arch near the tourist office and you will reach the town's active and characterful pannier market. Tavistock is only 10 miles (16km) from Plymouth, but with its weathered stone buildings it belongs to another world.

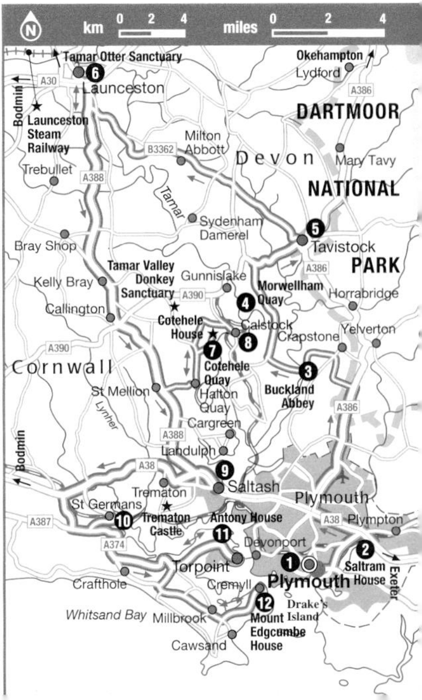

Above: Launceston Steam Railway runs along the lovely Kensey Valley.

LAUNCESTON

Take the B3362 about 12 miles (19km) northwest to **Launceston** ❻. Just 1 mile (1.6km) before the walled city you will cross the River Tamar into the county of Cornwall.

Launceston was Cornwall's principal town until civic power was transferred to Bodmin in 1835. A Victorian revival gave it a town hall and a guildhall, but its most interesting building is **St Mary Magdalene**, once the castle chapel and now the parish church. Go out via the North Gate into elegant 18th-century Castle Street. **Lawrence House Museum** (www.lawrencehousemuseum.org.uk; Apr–Oct Mon–Fri 10.30am–4-.30pm; free) was originally built in 1753 for a lawyer.

North of the centre is the **Launceston Steam Railway** (tel: 01566-775 665; www.launcestonsr.co.uk for exact hours and timetable; Easter and June–Sept, not Sat in peak season; charge). There is a museum, workshops and buffet and the old locomotives run 2.5 miles (4km) to Newmills.

THE TAMAR VALLEY

From Launceston, the A388, the major road south, deserts the Tamar, but our tour turns left at St Mellion and winds its way through pretty lanes to **Cotehele Quay** ❼. Evidence of a once busy trading place is captured in a museum, wharf buildings and the *Shamrock*, the last Tamar sailing barge. There's a National Trust tearoom, and a watermill, cider press and blacksmith's forge are a short walk through the woods.

Ⓥ Launceston Castle

Launceston Castle (Apr–June and Sept daily 10am–5pm, July–Aug until 6pm, Oct until 4pm; charge) sits in grounds immaculately maintained by English Heritage. The steep ascent to the keep is worthwhile for the astounding views from the top – not only of the town but also over Bodmin Moor and Dartmoor. William the Conqueror gave his half-brother, the Earl of Mortain, the land surrounding a hill site already fortified by Edward the Confessor and commanding the approaches to the west. Within a year the hill was crowned with the castle of Dunheved, a keep on an artificial motte, with bailey, walls and gates enclosing the settlement. Launceston was born, secure from English resistance.

Above: the lofty castle keep.

The complex relates to **Cotehele House** (NT; mid-Mar–Oct Sat–Thur 11am–4.30pm, daily in Aug; garden all year dawn–dusk; charge), a strong contender for the title of most beautiful stately home in the county. Built between 1485 and 1627, this great medieval building, hung with Flemish and English tapestries, is remarkably unchanged. In the chapel, a 15th-century clock, the earliest in England, still ticks, though it has no hands or pendulum.

A short riverside walk passes pretty Danescombe Hotel to **Calstock** ❽. River trade was ruined when the Tamar Valley railway line between Plymouth and Gunnislake was laid, but it gave the town one of the county's most attractive branch lines. The views of the river from the viaduct are breathtaking.

Until Victorian times **Gunnislake**, several miles upriver from Calstock, was the lowest bridging point on the Tamar. New Bridge, dating from 1520, was the scene of bitter fighting during the Civil War (1642–6).

Below: set in vast grounds, Cotehele House has a wonderful textile collection.

K Animal Rescue

Two children's animal favourites are accessible from Launceston. About 14 miles (22km) southeast is **Tamar Valley Donkey Park and Sanctuary** (tel: 01822-834 072; www.donkeypark.com; Easter–Sept daily 10.30am–5pm, Oct Thur–Sun 10.30am–4.30pm, Sat–Sun and school holidays in winter; charge). While north, off the A390 near Callington, you'll find the **Tamar Otter Sanctuary** (tel: 01566-785 646; www.tamarotters.co.uk; Easter–Oct daily 10.30am–6pm; charge).

Above: otters awaiting rehabilitation.

Above: the church of St Germans, a former priory and once Cornwall's cathedral.

SALTASH

Return to the A388 and drive south to **Saltash ❾**. Isambard Kingdom Brunel's magnificent Royal Albert Bridge straddled the Tamar in 1859 here, to bring broad-gauge railways into Cornwall, 9 miles (15km) south of Gunnislake. Not until 1961 did a new road bridge join Brunel's, forcing the closure of a ferry that had operated for 700 years. The new A38 took traffic around Saltash, leaving it to rest on its memories, the oldest ones embedded in the tiny Tudor cottage in Culver Road, where Sir Francis Drake's wife, Mary, was born. **Mary Newman's Cottage** can be visited as part of the Heritage Trail (Apr–Oct), as can Elliott's Grocery Store, a classic Saltash shop.

Stunning views can be had from below the bridge, where 18th-century houses cluster side by side with modern housing in the steep streets and on the quayside.

ST GERMANS

From Saltash, take the A38 westwards. High above a tidal creek of the Lynher River is **Trematon Castle**, an important Norman stronghold overlooking Plymouth Sound.

In Saxon times, the church at **St Germans ❿**, reached via a narrow left turn off the A38, was Cornwall's cathedral. After the bishops moved to Crediton, and later Exeter, it became an Augustinian priory, and the substantial remains of the Norman building are now the parish church.

Above: Brunel bridged the Tamar for the railways; the road bridge came later.

TWO GREAT HOUSES

The A38 joins the A374 to Torpoint and the Devonport ferry, passing **Antony House** ⓫ (NT; Apr–Oct Tue–Thur 1–5pm, also Sun June–Aug; woodland garden Mar–Oct Tue–Thur, Sat–Sun 11am–5.30pm; charge), by the River Lynher. Wings of red brick contrast with Pentewan stone and, although a little austere, it is one of the finest early 18th-century houses in Cornwall. Views of the river have been opened up in the 100-acre (40-hectare) park and woodland garden, landscaped by Humphry Repton.

From Antony House, head back to the main road junction and follow signs for **Millbrook**. From the village, at the head of a tidal creek, a delightful lane follows the waterside to **Mount Edgcumbe House** ⓬ (tel: 01752-822 236; www.mountedgcumbegov.uk; Apr–Sept Sun–Thur 11am–4.30pm; charge) and the entrance to the Country Park at Cremyll Ferry. The Edgcumbe family virtually abandoned their original home at Cotehele in favour of this new site overlooking Plymouth Sound.

Entrance to the 800-acre (320-hectare) park (all year daily) is free; it includes Cornwall's only Grade I listed historic garden, the National Camellia Collection, follies, grottoes, an orangery, a conservatory and a holy well.

There are dramatic coastal views from walks that lead to **Maker Church**, the tower of which served as a semaphore station in the 18th century. The coastal path soon descends to **Kingsand** and **Cawsand**, separated by a stream. In the early 19th century both subsisted on smuggling, for which their twisting, turning lanes seem to have been specially designed. From here it is just a short hop over the Tamar bridge to Plymouth.

Ⓔ Eating Out

Plymouth

Plymouth Canteen and Deli

Royal William Yard; tel: 01752-252 702; www.rivercottage.net; Tue–Sat breakfast (from 10am), lunch and dinner, Sun 9am–4pm, Mon in summer 10am–4.30pm.

Part of Hugh Fearnley-Whittingstall's River Cottage empire. Great local food, served canteen-style in a stunning waterfront building – carefully sourced produce is the key. £–££

The Waterfront

9 Grand Parade; tel: 01752-226 326; www.waterfrontplymouth.co.uk; daily noon–11pm.

Sit on the nautical deck on the Hoe and order a saucepan of Devon mussels poached in white wine, cream and shallots or home-baked fish pie. £–££

Tavistock

Brown's Wine Bar and Brasserie

80 West Street; tel: 01822-618 686; www.brownsdevon.co.uk; all day, daily.

In a former coaching inn, the hotel's smart restaurant, rooftop garden, orangery and comfortable lounges are perfect for lunch, cream tea or a special à la carte dinner. £–£££

Launceston

La Bouche Creole

Dockacre Road; tel: 01566-779 294; www.labouchecreole.co.uk; Thur–Sat dinner only 6.30–9pm.

Treat yourself at Cornwall's only Creole restaurant. With its fixed-price, changing menu and tempting dishes, such as gumbo made with local ingredients, this place is a winner. ££

Saltash

Bullers Arms

The Square, Landrake; tel: 01752-851 283; www.thebullersarms.com; daily lunch and dinner.

Friendly pub with an emphasis on local food where traditional pub favourites join specials such as hunter's chicken. £

Devon Tour 6

Dartmoor

One of Britain's great wilderness areas, Dartmoor is a high and haunting place. This 69-mile (111km) full-day drive reveals its mysteries and rugged grandeur.

Dartmoor National Park covers some 365 sq miles (945 sq km) of south-central Devon. Although the moor is governed by the park authority, the land is still largely in private hands. Prince Charles, title holder of the Duchy of Cornwall, is the largest single landowner. Look out for the Dartmoor ponies who have roamed here freely since the 10th century.

Reaching 2,037ft (621m), the moor is the highest land in southern England. Around half of it is open moorland, and the rest (particularly on the eastern side) is steep wooded valleys with secluded villages.

Dartmoor generates a climate of its own. In the distant past this climate was kinder, and the high moor was more heavily cultivated and populated than it is today. The first people worked the moor 10,000 years ago, and until 7,000 years ago it was mostly wooded. But as the climate worsened, so the population left their settlements in search of easier ground lower down. As a result, Dartmoor has a wealth of around 2,000 Bronze Age sites – hut circles, tombs and ceremonial stones – dating from around 4,000BC. Mixed in

Highlights

- Hay Tor
- Princetown
- Okehampton Castle views
- Museum of Dartmoor Life, Okehampton
- Lydford Gorge

Left: spectacular Hay Tor.

with Bronze Age remnants are signs of more recent industry, in particular the mining of tin, granite and copper from the 12th to 19th centuries.

Tin mining – largely tin streaming in the open river beds – was a boom industry, and the Dartmoor miners were granted special exemption from the nation's taxes. Although they never numbered more than a few hundred, they made a powerful group with their own laws, their own parliament (which met at Crockern Tor) and their own judiciary and prison at Lydford. Their contribution to the nation's coffers was made at the strategically placed stannary towns of Ashburton, Chagford, Plympton and Tavistock; here the tin was weighed and duty paid.

Strange legends and traditions persist, including the pastime of letterboxing, a sort of moorland treasure hunt *(see box p.51)*; and as recently as the mid-19th century, if you could build a house on Dartmoor between sunrise and sunset, it and the land were yours.

Since Napoleonic times areas have been assigned for military use. On firing days warning flags fly around restricted areas, and post offices and visitor centres display details of firing schedules.

F National Trust

If you are keen on visiting stately homes and, especially, gardens, it is worth considering becoming a National Trust member. Many of the houses and gardens described en route (those marked NT), and more besides, are in the care of the Trust. You could soon recoup your membership fee as well as contributing to the upkeep not only of the properties, but of much of the coast that is also under the Trust's protection.

Contact them at tel: 0844-800 1895, or www.nationaltrust.org.uk, or fill in a form and join on the spot when visiting any of their properties.

BOVEY TRACEY

The eastern gateway to the moor is **Bovey Tracey ❶**, a pleasant small town with a long main street heading up the hillside. It was the scene of an undignified fracas during the Civil War when Royalists were surprised at cards, but managed to escape by scattering their stake money, which proved too much of a temptation for Cromwell's impoverished troops.

From Bovey head west towards Widecombe. Just outside town is

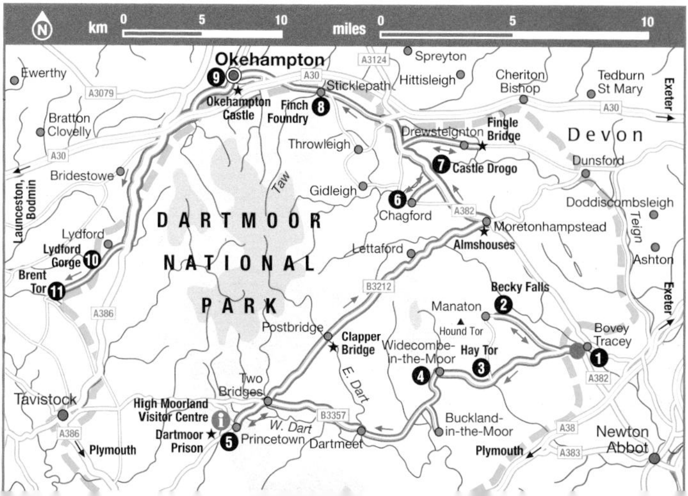

S Bovey Crafts

Bovey's solid granite architecture is unremarkable, but it does have two shopping highlights. In a small industrial estate on the Exeter side of town **The House of Marbles and Teign Valley Glassworks** has glass and pottery in a synthesis of museum and retailing, with some glass-blowing on site. Further towards the centre of town is the **Devon Guild of Craftsmen**, located in an appealing old riverside 'mill' (actually a stable block with a waterwheel to pump water for the horses), with exhibition space on the first floor. The range and quality of the Devon Guild's members is extremely high, but prices can be steep.

Above: pottery and glass items for sale.

Parke House, headquarters of the Dartmoor National Park Authority. At this point a short diversion northwest towards Manaton brings you to **Becky Falls** ❷ (charge), more a dramatic series of tumbles than a waterfall, with tearoom and nature trails in very pleasant woodland.

Above: St Pancras in Widecombe, the Cathedral of the Moor.

TO WIDECOMBE

Back on the Widecombe road, the climb is steep, and the moor opens out at the popular **Hay Tor** ❸ (1,491ft/450m), with far-reaching views. It is a short and relatively easy walk from the road to the great granite tor (rock). Running along the back shoulder of the hill is the **Granite Tramway**, a track made from granite, with points, that was used to transport granite from the quarry in the hillside 10 miles (16km) down to the Stover canal. To the northwest is **Hound Tor**, and in the valley on the far side are evident remains of a medieval village among the bracken.

Widecombe-in-the-Moor ❹ is a small, captivating place superbly situated in a deep trough but still 800ft (240m) above sea level. Its outsized church of St Pancras is known as the Cathedral of the Moor. The town has become a tourist attraction thanks to the song about its annual fair. It dates from the 1860s, and was intended to attract 'Uncle Tom Cobley and all' away from similar events elsewhere. Such is the power of advertising that the September fair remains a major celebration, with country skills and crafts.

Down narrow lanes south of Wide-

Above: beyond the lovely country lane lies eerie and impenetrable Dartmoor Prison, whose museum gives a glimpse of life inside.

combe are two other pretty Dartmoor villages. **Buckland-in-the-Moor**, although scattered around a wooded hillside, has one of the most photographed groups of thatched cottages in Devon. The small church has an unusual clockface with the 12 letters MY DEAR MOTHER instead of numerals. South still is **Holne**, birthplace of *The Water Babies* author Charles Kingsley. The 14th-century Church House Inn is one of Dartmoor's most characterful.

From Widecombe the main road heads west through the surprisingly popular spot of Dartmeet and thence up to Two Bridges. Both locations are little more than their names suggest: the former is the meeting place for the East and West Dart rivers, and the latter is a hotel next to old and new river crossings.

PRINCETOWN

Princetown ❺, the highest and bleakest settlement on Dartmoor, shelters beneath the huge transmitter mast on North Hessary Tor. It has the grim aspect of a frontier town, and in bad weather is regularly cut off. Amazingly, a railway reached here from Plymouth in 1883, but was closed in 1956.

After the mast, the town's landmark is **Dartmoor Prison**, built in 1806 for French prisoners of the Napoleonic Wars. After the introduction of deportation to the colonies it stood empty for many years, but today it functions as one of Britain's maximum security jails. A small **museum** (charge) charts

Above: a high point of Devon thatch at Buckland-in-the-Moor.

Above: hilltop Castle Drogo can experience extreme weather conditions.

its history, and has some confiscated items over the years. Its manager must be the only museum curator in the country liable to be called away in the event of prison riots.

Stories and legends

By Princetown's central crossroads is the **High Moorland Visitor Centre** (tel: 01822-890 414; www.dartmoor-npa.gov.uk; Apr–Sept daily 10am–5pm, Oct and Mar 10am–4pm, Nov–Feb Thur–Sun 10.30am–3.30pm, free; exhibition charge) with beautiful displays on Dartmoor's history and wildlife and insights into some of its legends. This is also the place to find out about the schedule of guided walks.

Across the road you'll find the ancient **Plume of Feathers**, the oldest building in the area (1795). During a refreshment stop here, you can ponder the story of the fearful winter wayfarer who opened a box seat in his room to discover the body of a man. Murder was assumed, until the landlord confessed that the body was that of his father, and he was only being stored there while the ground remained too hard to be dug.

From Princetown return northeast to Two Bridges and then north for **Postbridge**. This straight stretch of road has fuelled one of Dartmoor's best-known legends. A pair of hairy hands is reputed to have caused several accidents by appearing from nowhere and wresting control of the steering wheel. The 14th-century bridge at Postbridge, made from vast granite slabs, is the best

Above: the Three Crowns at Chagford is supposedly haunted by a Royalist poet who died in its porch.

Above: the old market hall, Chagford.

example of a traditional local 'clapper' bridge. The moor softens as the road continues northeast to **Moretonhampstead**, an attractive small town blighted by the five roads that meet in the town centre. Moreton has become something of an arts and crafts centre, with a number of studios and potteries. On the way out of town are Moreton's **almshouses**, dating from 1637 and the property of the National Trust.

CHAGFORD

Chagford ❻ lies a short distance northwest, off the A382 to Okehampton. Its stannary past has left the town looking remarkably elegant, gathered around a small market square at the centre of which is the six-sided and spired Market House (1862), known locally as the Pepperpot. Shopping around the square is a mixture of hardware and arts and crafts. Off the top left-hand corner of the square is the 16th-century Three Crowns hotel, which is supposedly haunted by the Cavalier poet, Sydney Godolphin, fatally shot here.

Back on the road to Okehampton, the silhouette of **Castle Drogo** ❼ (NT; tel: 01647-433 306; opening times vary, check www.nationaltrust.org.uk/castle-drogo; charge) looms ahead up on the hill to the right, although the journey to its door is about 3 miles (4.8km) through narrow lanes. This dramatic situation was chosen by one Julius Drewe while picnicking here with his family. Drewe, who had made his fortune in retailing, recruited the architect Edwin Lutyens, bought a nearby granite quarry, and thus the last castle

K Letterboxing

Dartmoor has something of a unique activity in letterboxing – an outdoor pursuit with similarities to orienteering, which older kids will enjoy. Some 2,000 'letterboxes', usually tin boxes, are hidden in remote locations over the moor. Walkers search out a particular letterbox (having first got the location from another letterboxer, or the letterboxing newsletter), stamp their own book with the letterbox's stamp, and then head on for the next. This occupation is so popular that over 1,000 letterboxers take to the moor every weekend.

Letterboxing began on Dartmoor but is now popular in areas all over the world. For information check out www.dartmoorletterboxing.org.

Above: letterboxers get a stamp to show they passed this way.

to be built in England was begun in 1910. The castle has plenty of features, including a wonderful bath, a dedicated power-generating system, and tapestries from the 17th century.

Outside are terraced gardens and woodland walks down into the Teign gorge. Particularly worthwhile is the walk to **Fingle Bridge**, a 400-year-old footbridge of some charm a couple of miles upstream, which can also be reached by road via the pretty hilltop village of **Drewsteignton**.

Just before Okehampton, in Sticklepath, is the **Finch Foundry** ❽ (NT; Apr–Oct daily 11am–5pm), remarkable because it was still manufacturing edged tools by hand as recently as 1960, using hammers, shears and grindstones powered by waterwheels – all still in working order. Local farmers swear by their Finch tools.

OKEHAMPTON

The A30 sweeps past the market town of **Okehampton** ❾, cutting it off from the moor to which it spiritually belongs. The town is a matter-of-fact sort of place, and is particularly well served by the **Museum of Dartmoor Life** (www.museumofdartmoorlife.eclipse.co.uk; Easter–Oct Mon–Fri 10.15am–4-.15pm, Sat 10.15am–1pm, shorter hours in winter; charge), found through an arch off the main street. The museum gives detailed insights into the archaeology and sociology of the moor, with good use of aerial photography.

Okehampton's **Castle** (tel: 01837-52844; Apr–Jun, Sep 10am–5pm, Jul–Aug 10am–6pm, closed Oct–Mar; charge) has been a ruin since Henry VIII seized it in 1538, but what it lacks in roof it makes up for in location, on a hilltop in a wooded valley half a mile

Above: the White Lady Waterfall in the scenic Lydford Gorge.

Above: mural in Okehampton depicting a man of the moor.

behind the museum, and with a riverside picnic area below. The castle was built in 1068 by Baldwin de Brionne, the first sheriff of Devon.

GORGE AND WATERFALL

Return to the A30 and then take the moor-skirting A386 south. Half way to Tavistock, off to the right, is the village of **Lydford**, a former administrative centre of the Royal Forest of Dartmoor whose castle is actually just a prison keep. The earth thrown up around it gives it the appearance of a castle.

The scenic **Lydford Gorge** ⑩ (NT; tel: 01822-820320; daily, mid-Mar–Oct 10am–5pm; charge) is just beyond the village. The river Lyd thunders through it, shadowed by an alarming walkway. In more gentle scenery downstream the river is joined by the elegant White Lady Waterfall, which is actually more a slide than a fall.

The last stop on this route, **Brent Tor** ⑪, can be reached either via back lanes from Lydford or by returning to the A386. From here it is a short distance to Tavistock *(see p.41)*.

E Eating Out

Widecombe-in-the-Moor

Rugglestone Inn

tel: 01364-621 327; www.rugglestoneinn.co.uk; daily lunch and dinner.
Sample good home-cooked fare washed down by a real ale or local farm cider at this pretty stone pub near the centre of Widecombe. It's wise to book in high season. £

Bovey Tracey

The Old Pottery

The House of Marbles; tel: 01626-835 285; www.houseofmarbles.com; Mon–Sat 9am–5pm, Sun 10am–5pm.
Located in The House of Marbles and Teign Valley Glassworks, this locals' favourite serves excellent brunch and Devon cream teas. Salads, sandwiches and traditional mains also feature. £

Princetown

The Plume of Feathers Inn

Yelverton; tel: 01822-890 240; www.theplumeoffeathersdartmoor.co.uk; daily lunch and dinner.
This atmospheric inn has a frequently changing menu with local Dartmoor meats from an award-winning butcher, and fresh Devon vegetables. There is also a carvery on Sundays, as well as a beer garden and a large, safe, fenced-in adventure play area. £

Chagford

Gidleigh Park

tel: 01647-432 367; www.gidleighcom/restaurant.html; daily lunch and dinner.
This two Michelin-starred property on the connoisseur and celebrity circuit, enjoys an idyllic setting on the banks of the North Teign River. With Head Chef Michael Caines at the helm, the restaurant is renowned for creating innovative European dishes using superb Devon produce. £££

Sandy Park Inn

tel: 0845-206 1557; www.sandyparkinn.co.uk; daily lunch and dinner (Sun lunch only).
Enjoy fine home-made food and gourmet pizzas at this thatched 17th-century inn near Castle Drogo, which can be seen from the terrace. £–££

Above: Gidleigh Park dessert.

Devon Tour 7

North Devon

Discover North Devon's popular resorts of Woolacombe and Ilfracombe, then continue westwards to charming Clovelly and the wild coast off Hartland Point.

This 77-mile (124km) tour will take you a full day if you are driving, more if you want to make the most of all the attractions en route.

Highlights

- Woolacombe Beach
- Ilfracombe
- Wildlife and Dinosaur Park
- Barnstaple Pannier Market
- Westward Ho!
- Clovelly
- Hartland Quay and Point

BRAUNTON

Our journey begins at **Braunton ❶**, where surf shops give a clue of what is to come and the Museum of British Surfing (Caen Street; tel: 01271-815 155; www.museumofbritishsurfing.org.uk; Tue–Sun 11am–5pm; charge), opened in 2012, charts the history of surfing and displays memorabilia. The flat land nearby is more interesting than it seems; what used to be RAF Chivenor is now a base for the Royal Marines, and beyond it is the Braunton Great Field, an ancient field system with divisions still visible. Penetrate down these lanes to **Braunton Burrows**, sand dunes known for their botany and birdlife, with views over the estuary. The whole area has been designated by Unesco as Britain's first Biosphere Reserve, because of its variety of habitats. Most visitors continue on to **Saunton**, an impressive stretch of beach, popular with sand-yachts, wind- and wave-surf-

Left: have your photo taken with a friend. **Above**: Braunton Burrows.

ers, although with limited access due to the golf club stretching along its back.

The road then girdles the headland to **Croyde Bay**, with holiday camps and an attractive beach, popular with both families and surfers – Croyde Bay provides one of the best surfing destinations in the UK, with good waves for experienced surfers. Lifeguards patrol the beach in summer.

Take the right turn up through the pretty village and on via a narrow road to **Georgeham**, shoe-horned into a narrow valley. This is where Henry

Tarka Line and Trail

Take a low-impact day out exploring Devon's rolling hills by train on the Tarka Line. Opened in 1854, it follows the river valleys of the Taw and Yeo from Exeter to Barnstaple. Tarka the otter, in Henry Williamson's famous tale of the same name, travels the same route. From Barnstaple station you can rent a bike and cycle the Tarka Trail, a traffic-free cycle path (Tarka Trail Cycle Hire; tel: 01271-324 202).

Above: take the Tarka Trail on the traffic-free cycle path.

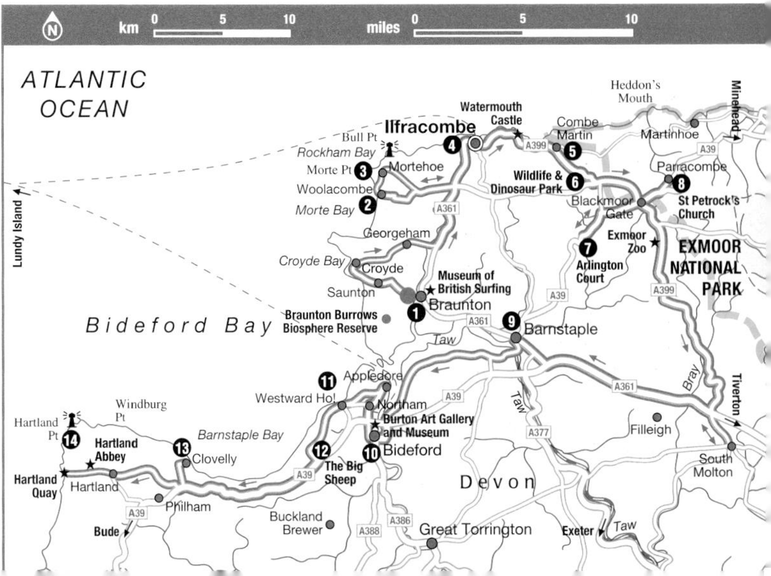

Williamson wrote *Tarka the Otter*.

From here, **Woolacombe ❷**, the finest beach in Devon, is tantalisingly close. Turn left, and the road descends gradually to the beach below. The beauty of Woolacombe is the uniform sand, the dunes and the green sward behind them. On non-beach days a fine alternative is to round the corner to Mortehoe, park the car and walk to **Morte Point ❸**, on a grassy headland with great cliff scenery.

ILFRACOMBE

The most important resort of the north is **Ilfracombe ❹**, although it lacks a beach of quality. A fishing village until the 19th century, its natural harbour brought steamer traffic and the railway. The tide of tourism rose quickly, and the population had doubled by 1860, and doubled again by 1891. But the high watermark had been reached: the tide has since receded, leaving the town fossilised between then and now.

Ilfracombe's location is a good one, and its unprepossessing main street up the hill away from the main tourism area, preserving the holiday enclave to which three small shoreline hills provide shelter. The most seaward (Lantern Hill) protects the characterful **port**. Lundy trips, sea fishing charters and seasonal coastal cruises aboard a paddle-steamer are offered here. Lantern Hill is crowned by **St Nicholas Chapel**, with neat whitewashed interior and all-round view.

At the foot of the third shoreline hill you'll reach the eccentric **Museum** (www.ilfracombemuseum.co.uk; Apr–Oct daily 10am–5pm, Nov–Mar Tue–

Above: Woolacombe has won awards for having the best beach in Britain.

Above: Ilfracombe, North Devon's principal resort, is in an incomparable setting; from there you can take boat trips to Lundy.

Fri 10am–1pm; charge). The collection charts the resort's heyday and includes plenty of oddities: a drawer full of old wedding cake, a two-headed kitten, and the Ilfracombe radio station.

The road east out of Ilfracombe rolls around the coast. It plunges down to sea level at **Watermouth Cove**, with its natural harbour. Watermouth Castle has been converted into a family theme park.

COMBE MARTIN

Combe Martin ❺ is not much more than a one-street town, but the street runs some 2 miles (3km) from the head of the valley to the sea. At the top of the valley is the **Wildlife and Dinosaur Park** ❻ (tel: 01271-882 486; www.dinosaur-park.co.uk; Feb half term–Nov daily 10am–5pm; charge), one of the premier attractions in the region, with full-size dinosaur models in the woods, an earthquake canyon train ride, plus wildlife including sea-lions, birds of prey and meerkats.

Combe Martin's most unusual building is the **Pack of Cards** pub, built by a gambler to resemble just that, with 52 windows and 52 doors.

On the far side of the bay, Little Hangman rises steeply out of the sea. There are fine walks up to its peak from the car park, and thence onto the shoulder of Great Hangman.

The A399 climbs inland from the town onto the fringes of Exmoor. Off to the right is **Arlington Court** ❼

Playtime in Ilfracombe

Parents with kids in tow will enjoy Ilfracombe's **Tunnels Beaches** complex (tel: 01271-879 882; www.tunnelsbeaches.co.uk; Apr–Oct daily 10am–6pm, check the website for early closing times; charge). After a dip in the tidal pools check out stylish Café Blue Bar. Here you can catch some rays on the deck, sip a glass of wine and have a bite to eat. For young kids there is a special menu and an indoor and outdoor soft play hut with a wooden pirate ship (charge). Older kids can surf the net or play on the large-screen iMac.

Above: the stunning garden and conservatory at Arlington Court.

(NT; mid-Mar–Oct daily 11am–5pm; charge), North Devon's only substantial country house open to the public. Built in 1822, it has a large carriage museum, and is imprinted with the character of its most recent owner, Rosalie Chichester, a grand dame and collector. Its superb parkland includes a heronry.

Also worth a detour, on the other side of the A399, is the tiny church of **St Petrock** ❽, on the upper edge of the nestled village of **Parracombe**. Parts of this church may be 13th century, but because it was supplanted by a newer church, it remains a relic of the 18th century, with hand-lettered scriptures on the screen, rickety pews and planking. Instructions for obtaining the key can be found at the church.

The A399 skirts the edge of the moor, with fine views off to the left, past the child-oriented **Exmoor Zoo** (www.exmoorzoo.co.uk; daily 10am–5pm, till 6pm May–mid-Sept, dusk in winter; charge), before dipping down into the lush Bray valley and thence to **South Molton**, a pleasant Georgian market town known for its antiques shopping. From here it's a 12-mile (20km) drive to Barnstaple on the A361.

BARNSTAPLE

Barnstaple ❾ is a farming town where industrial estates and shopping centres have bloomed in the past decade. The town has a long history. Pilton, a district to the west of the centre, received its royal charter in 930, making it one of the oldest burghs in England. Early success was due to Barnstaple's

Above: the Albert Memorial Clock in Barnstaple town square.

Above: meerkat at Exmoor Zoo.

position at the highest navigable and lowest crossable point of the River Taw, but silting up and the growth of Bideford put paid to serious trade.

Little remains of Barnstaple's origins. The Norman Castle, near the Civic Centre, is just a mound spiked with trees. The first bridge was built in 1273, and although it has been much altered since, you can still see the original brickwork if you take the riverside underpass at the east end. The town's strategic position was highlighted again at the beginning of the railway age when five lines converged here, of which only one remains. More recently, the arrival of the A361 link road brought another resurgence.

Penetrate through a narrow lane halfway down Butcher's Row near the **Pannier Market** *(see box below)* and you enter a hidden, grassy square with the unexceptional St Peter's Church to the right and the graceful **St Anne's Chapel** (1330) in the centre. The chapel has had many functions, and once housed the grammar school attended by poet John Gay.

The centre of town rather ignores Barnstaple's square, with its Albert Memorial Clock, but don't miss the **Museum** (Mon–Sat 9.30am–5pm; free), next to the bridge. Hands-on displays highlight wildlife, sea life, transport, industry and folklore of the area in an excellent, compact collection.

Just down river from the square is the colonnaded **Queen Anne's Walk** (1709), where merchants gathered to do their deals with the figure of the Queen above their heads. Upriver from the square, up Litchdon Street, you can admire the **Penrose**

S Barnstaple Pannier Market

A focal point of Barnstaple is the **Pannier Market** (tel: 01271-379 084; www.barnstaplepanniermarket.co.uk; Mon 9am–4pm, Tue–Sat 9am–3pm), housed in an 1855 building on the High Street. This is the best of Devon's many such markets, offering a wide range of fresh produce, handmade arts and crafts together with antiques and collectables. Organic fruit and vegetables are also on sale throughout the week in Butcher's Row, a colourful parade of shops that runs along the market flank.

Above: choose from Devon's many cheeses at the daily market.

Above: Bideford Quay, once the hub for imports of tobacco, wool and timber.

Almshouses (1627); linger within the quad and one of the residents might just give you a tour.

BIDEFORD

Continue out on the Bideford road, which eventually leaves the Taw estuary and swings left to meet the Torridge. Across the water are views of first Appledore, with its covered shipyard, and then **Bideford** ⑩ itself, with a jumble of houses and shops behind a pretty riverside quay.

The link-road bridge, high overhead, has released the pressure on Bideford's 24-arch bridge, much of which dates from 1535, but the quay remains the focus of town life. Bid-

G Lundy Island

Lundy Island is a lonely, peaceful 3-mile (5km) slice of high land 11 miles (18km) offshore where puffins well outnumber the resident population. Owned by the National Trust and managed by the Landmark Trust, Lundy is rich in curiosities and natural history. Activities include diving, climbing, birdwatching, fishing and snorkelling. There's a pub, shop and a variety of accommodation (including the old lighthouse). The MS *Oldenburg* sails to Lundy from Bideford and Ilfracombe (Apr–Oct). For more information, tel: 01271-863 636; www.lundyisland.co.uk.

Above: a Lundy puffin: breeding pairs have declined recently.

eford was once the third-largest port in Devon, and ships left here for the Americas, although shallow waters restricted significant later development. Today, most of the space is taken by fishing boats and leisure craft.

At the far end of the Bideford quay is Victoria Park, and the **Burton Art Gallery and Museum** (www.burton artgallery.co.uk; Mon–Sat 10am–4pm, Sun 11am–4pm; free), an arts space of great distinction and great aspirations, with a small museum upstairs and an education centre. The quay is also the mainland station for **Lundy Island** *(see box opposite)*.

Appledore is still fundamentally a fishing and boat-building village, with close-packed white cottages climbing the hill, and a small seasonal **maritime museum** (charge) up above, from where there are tremendous estuary views.

Around the corner facing the open sea is the Victorian resort town of **Westward Ho! ⓫**, its name borrowed from the epic novel by Charles Kingsley which is based on Bideford, home to Kingsley in the 1850s. The resort was created by a 19th-century development company who realised the potential of the 2 miles (3km) of sandy beach and extensive grasslands of Northam Burrows.

One of the most innovative of Devon's farm attractions is **The Big Sheep ⓬** (www.thebigsheep.co.uk; Apr–Oct daily 10am–6pm, limited winter opening; charge) at Abbotsham, just off the A39. Anything to do with sheep takes place here – lamb-feeding, shearing, sheepdog trials and even sheep racing.

CHARMING CLOVELLY

The A39 shadows the coast to just above **Clovelly ⓭** (tel: 01237-431 781; www.clovelly.co.uk; summer 9am–6.30pm, shorter hours in winter; charge), a perfectly preserved fishing village that flows like spilt paint down a steep hill to a small harbour.

The whole village is owned by the Clovelly Estate, purchased in 1738 by the Hamlyn family, who still live in Clovelly

Below: the Burton Art Gallery and Museum also contains a Tourist Information Centre.

Above: head to Hartland Point for absolutely glorious walking along the coast, complete with dramatic coastal views along the South West Coast Path.

Court at the top of the hill. There is a visitor centre by the car park at the entrance to Clovelly, and below it the village is remarkably unspoiled, with bumpy cobbles to negotiate in the walk down to the fishing cove (a Land-Rover service operates in season however).

Most of the village's income is derived from its 300,000 annual visitors, although fishing boats do still function. Charles Kingsley lived here *(see p.36–37)*, while his father was curate at the church, and a small Kingsley museum is adjacent to a preserved fisherman's cottage. The Clovelly lifeboat is still active, and a small museum is occasionally open to the public.

Below: Clovelly harbour at low tide.

HARTLAND POINT

This is undoubtedly a treacherous coast for ships, and nowhere more so than off **Hartland Point** ⓮, the last stop on this route. This is Devon's coast at its most wild.

Hartland's layout has been determined by the weather. Its lighthouse is right on the point, while the village, with a long, low main street, is a couple of miles inland. The manorial residence of **Hartland Abbey** (www.hartlandabbey.com; check website for opening times; charge) is tucked into a sheltered valley below the village of Stoke, on the way to Hartland Quay. The abbey remains date from 1157 and the main house from 1779. The Stucley family, who still own Hartland Abbey, have their own side chapel in **St Nectan's church** up above, which has the tallest tower (128ft/38m) in North Devon. St Nectan's bears the marks of its exposed position. Note the counter-weighted church gate.

From here it is a short descent to **Hartland Quay**, which today is little more than a hotel clinging to some of the finest cliff scenery in Britain. The quay was authorised by an act of Parliament back in 1586, and it was still functioning at the end of the 19th century, since when storms have smashed it to smithereens. This is a strikingly beautiful place, backed by massive cliffs with muscular veined strata, and likely to leave a lasting impression on the visitor who comes here on a stormy day.

Above: down the cobbled lanes of Clovelly through traditional white-washed cottages.

E Eating Out

Croyde

The Thatch
14 Hobbs Hill; tel: 01271-890 349; www.thethatchcroyde.com; daily.
Surfing dudes and sea dogs mingle merrily at this cob barn pub. Eats include ribs, steaks, seafood and Devon cream teas. £–££

Woolacombe

nc@ ex34
South Street; tel: 01271-871 187; www.noelcorston.com; daily lunch and dinner.
Chef Noel Corston has re-opened his award-winning Courtyard Restaurant with a new name and a new brasserie style. ££

Ilfracombe

The Quay
11 The Quay; tel: 01271-868 090; www.thequay.com; daily lunch and dinner.
Chic eatery with lovely views, owned by artist Damien Hirst whose fishy work is showcased here. Choose from the likes of Lundy crab claws and Exmoor "Angus" steak. £££

Barnstaple

Jalapeno Peppers
Maiden Street; tel: 001271-328 877; www.jalapeno-peppers.co.uk; daily dinner only.
Classic Mexican and Cajun dishes in a lively converted warehouse restaurant. Mexican beers and frozen margaritas served until midnight. £–££

Bideford

Hoops Inn
Horns Cross, Nr Clovelly; tel: 01237-451 2220; www.hoopsinn.co.uk; daily lunch and dinner.
Long, low thatched pub on the A39 between Bideford and Clovelly. Real ale and good seafood. Accommodation available. ££

Appledore

Bensons
20 The Quay; tel: 01237- 424 093; www.bensonsonthequay.com; Tue–Sat lunch, tea and dinner.
Small restaurant specialising in local fish which doubles as a tearoom in the afternoon. No children under 12. ££ (light lunch/cream tea £)

Devon Tour 8

Exmoor

Explore heather-covered moors and dramatic, beautiful coastline on this 67-mile (108km) full-day car and walking tour of Britain's second-smallest national park.

Exmoor National Park may be small at 265 sq miles (670 sq km) but it offers an incredible variety of landscapes and wildlife, with wild red deer and Exmoor ponies among its blanket bogs and valley woodlands. A quarter of the park is in Devon and the rest in Somerset, more extensively farmed than Dartmoor and with habitation more widespread. Its long history is charted in some Bronze Age remains: many hills are topped by Iron Age forts or Beaker period barrows, while Tarr Steps is finer than any 'clapper' bridge found on Dartmoor.

Highlights

- Lynmouth Cliff Railway
- Doone Valley
- Selworthy
- Dunster
- Dunkery Beacon

COMBE MARTIN

This tour begins from **Combe Martin ❶**, at the western edge of Exmoor. Be warned: the first section follows the dramatic coastline through steep and difficult roads, of which the first is a taste of what's to come: Shute Lane leaves Combe Martin's main street just down from the Pack of Cards pub, and rapidly climbs to such a height that Dartmoor can sometimes be seen on a clear day, to the south. On the left of the road is **Great Hangman ❷**, reached by footpath, with breathtaking cliff scenery.

Left: the magnificent coastline near Great Hangman. **Above**: enjoying the waters in the Doone Valley.

HOLDSTONE DOWN

After a couple of miles running parallel with the valley of Combe Martin, turn left at a junction signed to Trentishoe and Hunter's Inn. Shortly after the turning you'll pass the National Park sign. Here, too, the views continue, with the vale of Parracombe dropping down to the right, and the barren 1,146ft (344m) **Holdstone Down** with fine walking and cliff scenery rising up to the left.

The road then slips inland down into the thickly wooded Heddon Valley. At the bottom, the half-timbered **Hunter's Inn** is a popular refreshment stop and focal point for walks. Take the steep road alongside the inn signed to Martinhoe, and then go left towards Woody Bay at the next T junction. Following signs to Lynton, take the toll road up through the Lee Abbey estate. Looking down is the **Valley of the Rocks**, a dramatic land formation thought to have been created by the River Lyn.

LYNTON

The road climbs out of the valley and into the back of **Lynton** ❸, another Victorian development. George Newnes, publisher of the Sherlock Holmes stories, gave the town its grand Town Hall, where the tourist information office is located. Take a right down into Queen Street for the heart of the town. Round the corner at the bottom is the seasonal **Lyn and Exmoor Museum**, in a cob cottage.

Lynmouth's ❹ main attraction is its location. Its small harbour is guarded by the Rhenish Tower. The **Cliff Railway** *(see box p.66)* arrives on the seafront almost next to the **Exmoor Park Visitor Centre**, which includes a replica of the town's most famous life-

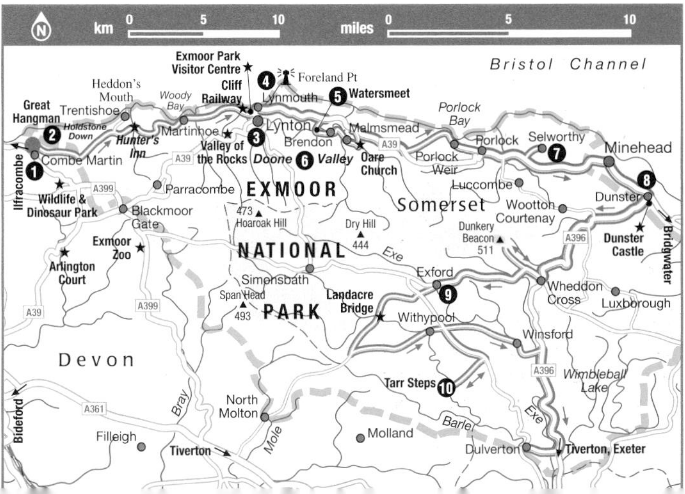

boat. The Lynmouth Pavillion has been acquired to house a new Exmoor Park Visitor Centre, due to open in 2013.

West from Lynmouth on the A39, **Watersmeet** ❺, a 19th-century fishing lodge turned into a tearoom and shop (National Trust), is a good place to start a walk, and from here you should head upstream. Walk up the East Lyn River and you'll emerge at Brendon, on the doorstep of the **Doone Valley** ❻. The actual story of R D Blackmore's *Lorna Doone* has become less well known than the region itself, dubbed Doone Country. Lorna and her hero John Ridd were married in **Oare Church**, where Blackmore's grandfather was vicar.

To travel to the valley by car, leave Lynmouth on the Porlock road up Countisbury Hill and once past County Gate (you are entering Somerset) take a right signed to Brendon. Turn left at the bottom for Malmsmead, and the pretty, winding valley climbs gradually into bandit country, marked by the attractive little **Robber's Bridge**. Return to the A39, and descend (the toll road has better views) to **Porlock**.

The Cliff Railway

Sherlock Holmes' publisher George Newnes financed the building of the **Cliff Railway** (tel: 01598-753 486; www.cliffrailwaylynton.co.uk; mid-Feb–mid-Nov daily 10am–5pm with exceptions; charge) which links Lynton with Lynmouth, 500ft (150m) below. The railway is worked by water. The car at the bottom discharges its 700 gallons until the weight of the top car is sufficient to pull it to the top, the most environmentally friendly way to travel. You can enjoy a beer, a snack and the awesome view at the Cliff Top Café.

Above: water-powered cable car.

SELWORTHY

Picture-book prettiness lies a little further east, in **Selworthy** ❼. Lying at the heart of the National Trust's Holnicote estate, the village was rebuilt in 1828 by Sir Thomas Acland of Killerton, who used traditional designs and materials to create a deliberately old-fashioned village of cream-washed stone thatched cottages to house the aged and infirm of the estate. Continue on to **Dunster** ❽, a well-preserved medieval town with a dramatic 19th-century **Castle** (Mar–Nov daily 11am–5pm) and 17th-century circular **Yarn Market**.

Our route turns inland, up the A396. After some miles turn right at Wheddon Cross, towards Exford. If the day is clear, branch right to **Dunkery Beacon**, Exmoor's highest spot at 1,704ft (511m). The Beacon rises gradually, the walk is easy, and from the top one can supposedly see 16 counties.

EXFORD

Exford ❾, sheltering in the Exe valley, is the heart of Exmoor and the centre for Exmoor recreation.

Cross the river bridge and turn left up the hill. At the top, go straight over the crossroads, through a ford to **Landacre Bridge**. Cross Landacre, climb

Above: Tarr Steps across the River Barle has been here for around 3,000 years.

out of the valley and turn left to **Withypool**. Follow the signs for **Tarr Steps** ⓾. Descend to the car park and walk down to this 17-span 'clapper' bridge, said to be up to 3,000 years old.

Back up on Winsford Hill, retrace your steps a mile or so and take a right down into the pretty village of **Winsford**, dominated by the Royal Oak Inn. The A396 runs to the east of Winsford. Head south, and turn off it at the signpost for **Dulverton**. This handsome farming town on the River Barle is where our Devonian journey ends.

E Eating Out

Combe Martin

Ye Olde George and Dragon

Castle Street; tel: 01271-882 282; www.georgeanddragon.uk.com; restaurant: daily lunch, Wed–Sat dinner.

Steaks sourced from Exmoor are a speciality at this recently refurbished restaurant, housed in the oldest pub in the village. £–££

Lynton

The Rockford Inn

Brendon; tel: 01598-741 214; www.therockfordinn.co.uk; Mon dinner, Tue–Sun lunch and dinner.

Take a pew by the river and enjoy real ale along with game pie or a bowl of River Exe mussels. Popular with local farmers, fishermen and ramblers. £–££

Lynmouth

The Rising Sun

Harbourside; tel: 01598-753 223; www.risingsunlynmouth.co.uk; daily lunch and dinner. ££

Loved locally for its high standards, its simple menu draws on local game and seafood. RD Blackmore wrote some of *Lorna Doone* here; the poet Shelley is believed to have honeymooned here and Coleridge stayed too. ££

Porlock

The Café

Porlock Weir; tel: 01643-863 300; www.thecafeporlockweir.co.uk; food served Wed–Sun 12am–8pm.

Set in front of the 13th-century harbour, The Café, formerly known as "Andrews on the Weir", delivers thanks to talented chef Andrew Dixon. ££

Dulverton

Tarr Farm

Tarr Steps; tel: 01643-851 507; www.tarrfarm.co.uk; daily, all day.

A converted 16th-century farm, next to the ancient 'clapper', is now a traditional restaurant committed to using local suppliers. ££

Cornwall Tour 9

The South Coast Harbours and Bodmin Moor

This 74-mile (120km) tour explores the pretty south coast harbours – Looe, Polperro, Polruan and Fowey – then heads inland to Bodmin Moor and the fabulous Eden Project.

This tour encompasses many of Cornwall's gems and should ideally be done over a couple of days – if not three – to give them the time and attention they deserve. Look at our Accommodation pages *(see p. 124)* for our recommendations in the area.

Highlights

- Liskeard
- East Looe
- Polperro
- Fowey
- Bodmin Moor
- Lanhydrock
- Eden Project
- Lost Gardens of Heligan

LISKEARD

Liskeard ❶ (on the A38 from Saltash) still has much to offer in the wealth of its Georgian buildings, second only to Truro. **St Martin's** is a plain, no-nonsense church, the Victorian **Guildhall** is Italianate with a clock tower. There are imposing stone and slate-hung houses in The Parade, a Regency **Market Hall**, and Stuart House, where Charles I slept for nine nights during the Civil War (1642–6). Well Lane has a surprise attraction – although it looks as if it wants to keep it hidden: in an arched grotto, water, once believed to

Left: the quays of East Looe are lined with trawlers. **Above**: tourism money is vital to the town's prosperity.

have curative properties, spouts from the 16th-century **Pipe Well**.

Unexpected pleasures

Take the B3254 south, which hugs the railway and the old Liskeard–Looe Canal as far as St Keyne Station and **Magnificent Music Machines** ❷ (tel: 01579-343 108; www.paulcorinmusic.co.uk; May–Oct daily 10.30am–5pm). Housed in a water mill, the great Wurlitzer and the other organs strike a fascinating note.

A lane opposite climbs up to **St Keyne's Well**, famous for giving a person who drank from it mastery over their spouse in marriage. Join the A387 and continue south to Looe.

EAST AND WEST LOOE

A deeply wooded valley joins that of the West Looe River, above the bridge that links East and West Looe, which were both given charters in the 13th century. **East Looe** ❸ is the larger and more commercially important; although its glory has faded, it's an attractive little town. The quays from which ore was loaded onto schooners now throng with visitors, and warehouses have been converted into holiday flats, restaurants and shops. The town's prosperity depends on tourism and on a revival of the fishing industry, whose trawlers line the quay. The 16th-century **Old Guildhall** (Mar–mid-Oct daily 11am–4pm; charge) houses a museum devoted to fishing and smuggling.

Across the bridge in **West Looe**, the 14th-century **Church of St Nicholas** on the quay has had a chequered career as a guildhall, prison and school. The **Jolly Sailor Inn** looks well adapted to its smuggling history.

POLPERRO

The drive to **Polperro** ❹ along the A387 is short and scenic. Polperro lives up to its reputation as Cornwall's most picturesque fishing village and though it never produced a recognised artists' colony, thousands of amateur artists come here to paint. Colour-washed cottages, some more than 300 years old, crowd the steep hillsides, converging on a brook that flows fast through the village, under

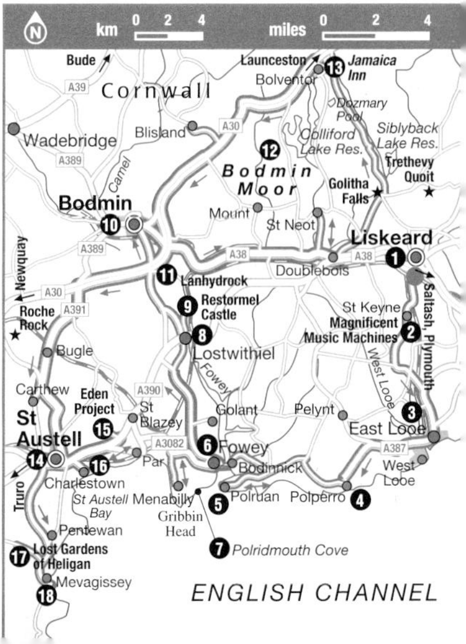

Ⓥ Fowey from Polruan

Polruan lives on its magnificent views from the pretty cottages above the tiny harbour and passenger ferry. Because of a threat from French marauders in 1457, it has a blockhouse built on the rocks at the shore, the twin of one at Fowey. **Hall Walk**, with panoramic views of Fowey, is reached from Pont Pill Creek and follows the hillside. It is especially stunning in March and April when the daffodils carpeting the river banks are in bloom.

Above: the waterside blockhouse at Polruan matches the one at Fowey.

stone bridges into the tiny harbour. Here, the **House on Props**, a 16th-century inn, is poised over the Roman – some say Saxon – bridge.

Cars are banished to the car park near Crumplehorn Mill Inn at the entrance to the village. In summer Gypsy-style carts wait to take visitors to the harbour and the Polperro-in-miniature **Model Village and Railway** (tel: 01503-272 378; Easter–Oct daily 11am–6pm; charge).

The **Heritage Museum of Smuggling and Fishing** (tel: 01503 272 423; Mar–Oct daily 10.30am–6pm; charge) sits on the quayside, and trips on fishing trawlers are offered from the Harbour Master's office. Take a path up the hillside to enjoy the splendid views.

POLRUAN AND THE FERRY

Polruan ❺ is Fowey's poor relation, declining as the town across the estuary prospered. From here follow the signs to **Bodinnick Ferry**, where car ferries make the two-minute crossing to Fowey at frequent intervals. 'Ferryside', on the waterfront, was once the home of novelist Daphne du Maurier, the author of *Rebecca* and *Jamaica Inn*. It is still the property of her family.

FOWEY

Houses huddle daintily around the deep-water harbour at **Fowey ❻** (pronounced *Foy*), which calls itself 'Du Maurier Country' and has a Du Maurier Literary Centre on South Street that can be visited (tel: 01726-833 616 for details). The Fowey estuary is one of the south coast's best sailing areas,

but also has romantic creeks for landlubbers to explore, along with some upmarket little shops and galleries for them to spend their money in.

In Trafalgar Square, the little **Fowey Museum** (Mon–Fri 10am–5pm; charge) has a history of its very own: built in 1792, it incorporates a 14th-century chapel, did time as a prison and now charts Fowey's maritime past.

POLRIDMOUTH COVE AND MENABILLY

Polridmouth Cove ❼ (pronounced *Pridmouth*) can be reached from the Fowey–St Austell road and a small car park. A short walk downhill will take you to the cove and a landlocked pool below the woods of **Menabilly**. To this place of haunted beauty Daphne du Maurier came in 1943, leaving reluctantly 24 years later when her husband died and the owner refused to renew her lease.

F Fowey History

Fowey had its time of glory seven centuries ago. When London could muster only 25 ships for the Siege of Calais in the Hundred Years' War, Fowey sent 47 ships and 700 men. Given a taste for action, these 'Fowey Gallants' turned pirates and carried on fighting even when the war was over. On one of their forays the French were unable to take **Place House**, the seat of the Treffry family, having failed to take account of the feisty resistance of Dame Elizabeth Treffry; although her husband was away fighting in the wars, she took them on and forced them to beat a hasty retreat. Today, the fairy-tale turrets and battlements of the largely 19th-century house provide the town with a peaceful and romantic backdrop.

Below: Polperro lives up to its reputation and paths winding up the hill offer splendid views over the picturesque harbour.

LOSTWITHIEL

It's difficult now to believe that **Lostwithiel** ❽ (reached via the B3269 from Fowey, or the faster A390) was once Cornwall's capital, the centre of the tin industry and a flourishing port. Yet its historic presence is still there, half-hidden in this serene, French-looking place beside the River Fowey.

In Quay Street are the remains of Stannary Court, the 14th-century **Duchy Palace**, which served as the Hall of the Exchequer, Shire Hall and prison. There are also numerous attractive 18th-century buildings, including in Fore Street the former **Corn Exchange**. It houses the Lostwithiel Museum (Apr–Sept Mon–Sat 10.30am–4.30pm; free), which evokes life during the 18th and 19th centuries.

Next stop is the 13th-century **Restormel Castle** ❾ (tel: 01208-872 687; Apr–June and Sept daily 10am–5pm, July–Aug until 6pm, Oct until 4pm; charge). The circular keep over the artificially steepened hill and a deep moat (now dry) was regarded as a perfect military solution.

GATEWAY TO THE MOOR

Bodmin ❿, gateway to the Moor, is reached via the A30 from Launceston or Truro, or the B3268 from Lostwithiel. It was on the old trade route from Ireland to the continent, and attracted 5th-century Christians who often broke their lengthy journeys here.

Guron was the first, as evidenced by his holy well in St Petroc's churchyard and a roadside fountain. St Petroc, Cornwall's senior saint, followed in the 6th century, founding a priory of which only fragments remain. The 15th-century **Church of St Petroc** (Apr–Sept daily 11am–3pm) has an important treasure: the cask that contained his relics. It has twice been stolen and returned, but without its contents. St Petroc's is Cornwall's largest church and its beautiful Norman font, supported by angels, is probably the best in the county. The church has good acoustics and is used as a venue for concerts.

Exploring the town

This sensible, hardworking town lost much of its administrative importance

Above: the manicured, landscaped Lanhydrock parkland.

Ⓚ Restormel Castle Picnic Spot

The wooded valley above the bridges of Lostwithiel is commanded by 13th-century **Restormel Castle**. Fought over in the Civil War, it survives as an impressive ruin and the grounds make a delightful picnic spot and a place for children to play. Pick up some pasties from Fran's Pantry (1A Quay Street, Lostwithiel). And try some of their local cheeses: Yarg, Davidstow Cheddar, Cornish Organic Brie, a local Goat's Brie and Cornish Blue.

Above: a place to spread out a rug and open a picnic hamper.

when its county town status was lost to Truro. The imposing, 19th-century **Shire Hall** (housing a helpful tourist office) stands in Mount Folly Square. The Tudor guildhall next door is now **Bodmin Museum** (tel: 01208-77067; Apr–Sept Mon–Fri 10.30am–4.30pm, Sat 2.30–4.30pm; free); it contains a manual fire engine, a Cornish kitchen and world war memorabilia, but won't detain you for long.

Some of the nation's most precious possessions, such as the Domesday Book (1086) and the crown jewels, were kept for safety during World War I in **Bodmin Jail** (tel: 01208-76292; www.bodminjail.org; daily 10am–dusk; 'paranormal walks' on specific dates), in Berrycombe Road. Public executions were held here in the middle of the 19th century; you can visit the dungeons for more gruesome details (charge).

The town's close links with the Cornish Infantry regiment are illustrated in the **Regimental Museum** (www.cornwalls-regimentalmuseum.org; Mon–Fri 9am–5pm; charge) in The Keep on the Lostwithiel Road.

Almost opposite is the station of the **Bodmin and Wenford Steam Railway** (tel: 01208-73555; www.bodminandwenfordrailway.co.uk; Feb–Dec, check for train times; charge). It has a refreshment room and souvenir shop and offers special events, as well as a nostalgic 6-mile (9km) trip.

LANHYDROCK

Bodmin's bypass (to the south) skirts the impressive 30-acre (12-hectare) parkland of **Lanhydrock** ⓫ (NT; tel: 01208-265 950; Apr–Sept Tue–Sun 11am–5.30pm, Mar and Oct until 5pm; park and gardens all year, daily; charge). The Robartes family lived here for more than 300 years, and the

Above: Restormel Castle.

Above: there are plenty of vestiges of the tin industry on Bodmin Moor.

National Trust has managed to retain a lived-in atmosphere.

THE MOOR

Travel eastwards on the A38 then north on a minor road to reach **Bodmin Moor ⓬**. This is a place to be treated with respect. Covering Cornwall's backbone in a granite blanket, it was home and shelter to the county's earliest inhabitants, and everywhere on the rock-strewn uplands are prehistoric stone circles, huts, barrows and medieval fields.

The bogs and heather of Bodmin Moor reach down the Loveny Valley to the road to Liskeard and **Carnglaze Slate Caverns** (tel: 01579-320 251; www.carnglaze.com; tours: Mon–Sat 10am–5pm, Aug until 8pm; charge), with the most beautiful pool hidden in its depths.

St Neot, higher up the valley, has royal connections. The saint was King Alfred's brother and his church is a wonder of light and colour; 15 windows shine with stained glass that is among the finest in England. At Doublebois, a road forks left to join the Fowey River at **Golitha Falls** in a National Nature Reserve and, passing **King Doniert's Stone** – with a Latin inscription to Dungarth, King of Cornwall – allows access to the **Siblyback Lake**. Here there are water sports and those with a day ticket may fish for trout. **Trethevy Quoit**, easily accessible nearby, is a magnificent example of a Neolithic tomb.

Above: the Cheesewring granite tors, perched above a quarry.

Above: poetic Dozmary Pool.

Still following the river upstream, **Dozmary Pool** lies to the left in the wildest part of the moor. In Alfred Lord Tennyson's poetic vision, it was here that King Arthur's sword was consigned to the waters after his death.

At Bolventor is **Jamaica Inn** ⓭, which does its best to live up to the character conferred on it by Daphne du Maurier's romantic novel. The slate-hung Georgian buildings look as if they could still harbour smugglers *(see p.125 for accommodation details)* and there is a small smugglers' museum attached (mid-Feb–Dec daily 10am–5pm, with exceptions; charge).

LEAVING THE MOOR

To the right of the A30, as you leave the moor, is **Blisland**. The Norman church (John Betjeman's favourite), with a brilliantly coloured screen and barrel roof, sits beside the only village green in Cornwall, an inn, a manor house and some cottages. Bypassing Bodmin, the A391 plunges into the much-abused landscape of china clay country *(see box below)*. At Bugle, a diversion can be made to **Roche Rock**, a granite outcrop capped with the 15th-century St Michael's Chapel and a hermit's cell below, reached by a ladder.

St Austell ⓮ is the area's main town. The town centre has been regenerated but the old quarter, the Market Hall and tower of Holy Trinity Church, offer good photo opportunities.

F Lunar Landscape

Approaching St Austell you will see the landscape has been transformed by the extraction of china clay, with stark white spoil heaps and water-filled pools giving it a lunar appearance. Not pretty, but the industry used to be a mainstay of the economy. A Plymouth chemist, William Cookworthy, discovered the clay near Helston in 1746. Its exceptional purity made it ideal for the production of porcelain and paper, and demand encouraged investment in the construction of ports at Par and Charlestown. **Wheal Martyn China Clay Museum** (tel: 01726-850 362; www.wheal-martyn.com; daily 10am–5pm with exceptions; charge), in the 26-acre (10-hectare) China Clay Country Park at Carthew, 2 miles (3km) north of St Austell, includes a disused works and brings the industry vividly to life.

Above: old clay works at the museum.

Above: waiting for the fish to bite in Charlestown.

Elsewhere are some fine old buildings, such as the White Hart Hotel and the **St Austell Brewery Visitor Centre** in Trevarthian Road (www.staustellbrewery.co.uk; Mon–Sat 10am–5.30pm, Sun Aug only; for tours, tel: 01726-66022; charge).

THE EDEN PROJECT

At Bodelva, signposted from the A391 before you reach St Austell, you'll find Cornwall's most spectacular and well-marketed attraction, the **Eden Project** ⓯ *(see feature, p.78)*.

Below: expect stunning flora at the Lost Gardens of Heligan.

CHARLESTOWN

Take the A390 past St Austell and follow signs to the port of **Charlestown** ⓰, the brainchild of Charles Rashleigh of Menabilly. Dug out of the beach in the 1790s, it has a granite-lined entrance and was intended for the shipment of both copper and tin. Today it handles china clay and sometimes caters for film crews. An inn or two, terraces of granite Georgian houses, stores and fish cellars provide the setting, and the **Charlestown Shipwreck and Heritage Centre** (tel: 01726-69897; www.shipwreckcharlestown.com; Mar–Oct daily 10am–5pm; charge, children under 10 free) tells the history of the town on both land and sea.

THE LOST GARDENS OF HELIGAN

The B3273 towards Mevagissey takes you to another of Cornwall's greatest attractions (also by Tim Smit of the Eden Project), the award-winning **Lost Gardens of Heligan** ⓱ (tel: 01726-845 100; www.heligan.com; daily Apr–Sept 10am–6pm, Oct–Mar 10am–5-pm; charge). These Victorian gardens became completely overgrown after the house was converted into a military hospital, and decades of neglect were compounded by the Burns' Day storm of 1990. The grounds are now beautifully restored, with boardwalks through a subtropical area, lakes, wetlands and woodlands in the Lost Valley, and vegetables and exotic fruits in the walled garden. There is also a pioneering Wildlife Interpretation Centre, where 'live' images of Heligan wildlife are displayed on plasma screens. Be aware that there is little shelter if the weather is bad.

Above: as made famous by the novel.

MEVAGISSEY

Pilchards were once the mainstay of **Mevagissey** ⓲, about a mile downhill from the Heligan turning. 'Mevagissey Ducks', as they were called, were salted in barrels to victual the Royal Navy, and supported a fishing fleet that both filled the large double harbour and in fed a flourishing community.

The little **Mevagissey Museum** (tel: 01726-843 105; www.mevagisseymuseum.co.uk; Easter–Oct daily 11am–5pm, 10am–5pm July and Aug; free), housed in an 18th-century boat yard on East Quay, has an interesting collection of old photos and marine artefacts.

E Eating Out

Looe

Terrace Restaurant at Talland Bay

Talland Bay; tel: 01503-272 667; www.tallandbayhotel.co.uk; daily lunch and dinner.

This award-winning country-house-style restaurant offers everything freshly made, from Cornish crab salad to seared fillet of bream. Bread and pasta are made on site too. There's a Sunday lunch menu that's popular with the locals – always a good sign. £££

Polperro

Nelson's

The Saxon Bridge, Big Green; tel: 01503-272 366; Tue–Sun dinner, Sun morning coffee, brunch and lunch.

Situated on the River Pol, Nelson's specialises in seafood and also offers vegetarian and gluten-free menus. Bookings essential in the restaurant but not in the adjacent Captain Nemo Bistro and Bar. £–££

Fowey

Food For Thought

4 Town Quay; tel: 01726-832 221; www.foodforthought.fowey.com; daily lunch and dinner, may close in winter.

First-class fish and seafood dishes, and equally good meat. ££–£££

Q Restaurant

28 Fore Street; tel: 01726-833 302; www.theoldquayhouse.com; daily lunch and dinner, closed lunch Sept–May.

Waterfront location with a smart interior. Local produce features, including Fowey river oysters. ££–£££

St Austell

The Lost Gardens of Heligan Tearoom

Pentewan; tel: 01726 845100; www.heligan.com; daily 10am–6pm, 5pm in winter.

Open to all, this award-winning café serves Cornish cream teas, and soups and salads that use produce from its Victorian restorative garden. £–££

The Eden Project

'A global garden, an environmental educational tool, an art gallery, a playground and an adventure' – the Eden Project is Cornwall's most popular attraction.

When record producer Tim Smit inaugurated his giant conservatories, the biomes, he, along with an influx of new industries and large investments, ushered in a new era in Cornwall's history.

GREEN TECHNOLOGY

'The decline of industry in the 19th century affected Cornwall in a profound way,' explains chief executive Smit. When mining died it created a melancholy mood. But because of Cornwall's historical links with industry it was ready to embrace new technology, particularly green technology. What blossomed turned out to be a dawning of a post-industrial revolution.

The project, a 35-acre (14-hectare) site in a disused clay pit, has transformed one of the few unattractive areas of Cornwall into a place everybody wants to visit. It is a vast global garden, incorporating huge, dome-shaped biomes that resemble a surreal space station made of bubble-wrap.

BIOMES AND BEYOND

In the **Rainforest Biome**, the world's largest greenhouse, full of tropical plants, there is much to be learned

Eden Information

The Eden Branchline bus service connects the Eden Project with St Austell station, and there are daily buses from Newquay. Tourist information centres and many hotels sell advance tickets (only groups can book in advance) for the same price as on the door, enabling you to get in faster on busy days. While this doesn't avoid the queues to get into the car parks, these have improved since the system was streamlined.

On arrival, you are shepherded into one of the car park tiers, which are 'fruit coded' – from cherries and plums near the top to apples at the bottom; a park and ride system operates from the higher levels. Come by bike and you pay a reduced entry price. There's an informative Visitor Centre, a large shop and several good cafés and restaurants, with lots of outdoor seating, as well as a little 'landtrain' pulled by a tractor run on biofuel that ferries people between the Visitor Centre and the biomes. For further information, and details of a packed year-round schedule of events (including ice-skating in winter), tel: 01726-811 911, or visit www.edenproject.com; daily June–Oct 9am–6/8pm, Nov–May 10am—4pm, with exceptions; charge.

about the coffee, banana and spice industries on mini plantations.

Inside the giant **Mediterranean Biome**, which re-creates the landscapes of the Mediterranean, California and South Africa, and the outdoor gardens, the crops – from olives and grapes indoors to hemp and sunflowers outside – are flourishing. And various growing systems are illustrated with models.

It is a place with serious environmental ambitions and there's a strong emphasis on education. Environmental lectures are conducted in the biomes, and an Education Centre is designed according to Fibonacci's sequence, one of nature's basic building blocks, using fully sustainable materials. On the lower floor are exhibits which show how plant energy powers the world and their ecosystems provide goods and services.

Above: space-age biomes in what was once an unsightly clay pit hold a wonderland of plants from around the world. **Top Left and Left**: fun plant sculptures help to make this a family-friendly attraction.

Kids Zone

The landscape at Eden is engineered to encourage curious young minds to explore their creativity in a playful way, with specific features dotted about to attract children of all ages.

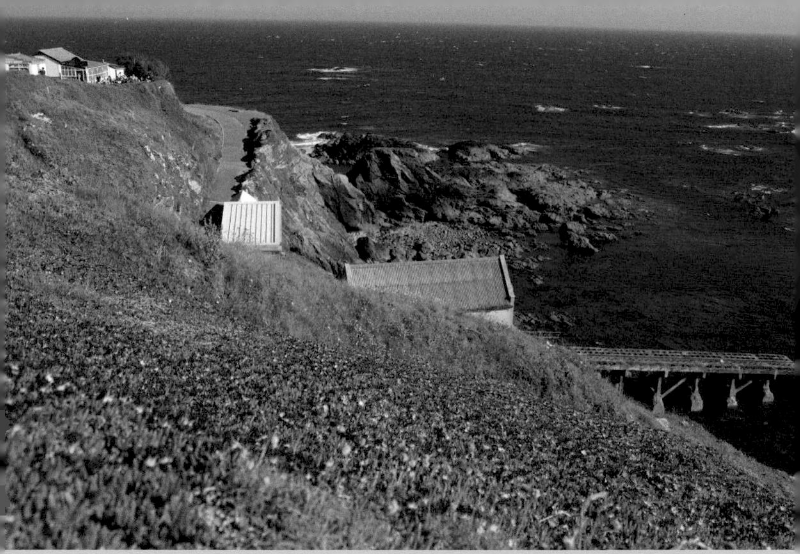

Cornwall Tour 10

Truro to the Lizard

This 84-mile (135km) drive starts in the cobbled streets of Truro, trips down the tiny lanes to Falmouth, then continues on to the untamed Lizard and Land's End.

Highlights

- Trelissick Gardens
- Falmouth and the National Maritime Museum
- Glendurgan Garden
- Trebah Garden
- Kynance Cove

TRURO

Truro ❶ is unquestionably a city, albeit a small one, but its aspirations are evident in the 1980s Crown Court building, by Eldred Evans and David Shalev who went on to design Tate St Ives. Added to this are a handful of restaurants, cafés, funky bars and imaginative shops recently opened in the centre.

The **Cathedral**, also in the centre of town, was begun in 1880, four years after the diocese of Truro was created. Opposite are the **Assembly Rooms**, although Truro's best building is only skin-deep: the 1772 interior no longer exists.

In nearby Boscawen Street, the **City Hall** houses the splendid Hall for Cornwall, a venue for concerts, theatre, dance and light entertainment. Opposite, the ancient Coinage Hall has a pizzeria on the ground floor and the idiosyncratic **Charlotte's Tea Rooms**, surrounded by rooms full of antiques, upstairs. Don't miss a cream tea in this delightful Victorian setting.

On the other side of Boscawen Street, the past is well documented in the **Royal Cornwall Museum** (www.royalcornwallmuseum.org.uk;

Ⓕ Truro's Changing Fortunes

The Normans were Truro's first settlers but the name Castle Hill is all that survives of their fort. Trade in tin brought prosperity and, in 1307, Truro became one of Cornwall's four regulators of the mining industry. Its fortunes sank as the market in tin fluctuated, and it wasn't until the 18th-century copper boom that the town thrived again. With the arrival of the railway in 1859, Truro's distinguished future was secured.

Above: the arrival of the railway secured Truro's economy.

Left: Lizard Point.

Mon–Sat 10am–4.45pm; charge, child free) in River Street. Its collection of archaeology, social history and art works from the Newlyn and St Ives Schools makes it one of the best museums in Cornwall.

TOWARDS THE ROSELAND PENINSULA

From Truro, the tree-shaded riverside road down the left bank of the River Truro climbs to the Heron Inn and the hanging gardens of **Malpas ❷**, with enchanting views of river and creek and quiet anchorages, once active with shipbuilding.

To reach the Roseland Peninsula, backtrack on the A390 and turn off just after **Tresillian** on the A3078. The road goes through **Tregony**, a sea port until the 17th century when the River Fal silted up with mush from the tin mines and clay pits. A left turn leads to the miniature fishing cove of **Portloe** where a stream reaches the beach from beneath the Lugger Hotel.

ST MAWES

Back on the A3078, take the left fork as you approach **St Mawes ❸** and follow the coastal road, past villas with

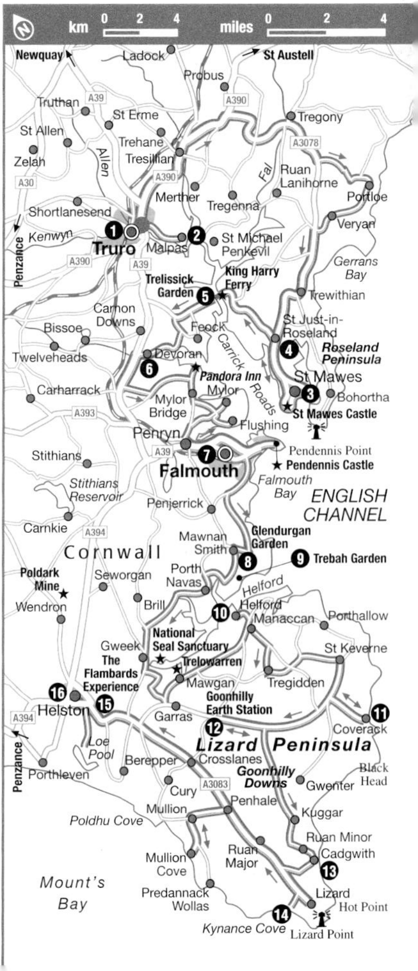

Unusual Gardens

Cornwall is known for its benevolent climate which suits many unusual plant species, and, with over 60 gardens to visit, it's easy to find examples. A trip from Tresillian, off the A390, takes you to **Trewithen** (www.trewithengardens.co.uk; Mar–Sept Mon–Sat 10am–4.30pm, Apr–May daily; charge). Here you'll see superb rhododendrons and more, with many of the plants propagated up for sale. The camera obscura is a fascinating addition.

lush, Mediterranean-style gardens, to the harbour. Pretty cottages, some thatched, line the seafront to the perfectly preserved **St Mawes Castle** (English Heritage; Sun–Fri, Apr–June and Sept 10am–5pm, July–Aug 10am 6pm, Oct 10am–4pm, Nov–Mar Sat–Sun 10am–4pm with exceptions; charge). Built in 1543, it is the best preserved of Henry VIII's defensive forts.

Above: the churchyard at St-Just-in-Roseland offers great views.

Leaving the village, take a left turn to **St Just-in-Roseland** ❹, where the lych gate of the church frames what is possibly Cornwall's most beautiful view. Reflected in St Just Pool, the 13th-century church makes a pleasing composition.

TRELISSICK GARDEN

The road back to Tregony invites exploration of backwaters: **Ruan Lanihorne**, which once had riverside wharves; and **St Michael Penkevil**, where the church and estate cottages cluster round the gates of Tregothnan, seat of the Boscawens, Earls of Falmouth. However, we take a more direct route to Trelissick and Falmouth on the B3289 from St Just, and board the King Harry Ferry, which makes the short trip across the Fal at 20-minute intervals (tel: 01872-862 312; www.falriver.co.uk for details).

Trelissick House, Grecian-style with a columned portico, is private, but **Trelissick Garden** ❺ is open to the public (NT; daily, mid-Feb–Oct 10.30am–5.30pm or dusk, Nov–mid-Feb 11am–4pm; charge). Among the National Trust's finest in Cornwall, the garden covers 25 acres (10 hectares) and is famous for hydrangeas and camellias. There is a lovely woodland walk.

DEVORAN TO PENRYN

At **Devoran** ❻ on Restronguet Creek (B3289 from Trelissick) are the grass-covered wharves and converted stores of a ghost port. Once connected by tramline with the mining area of Redruth, exporting minerals and importing coal, it survives on the sheer beauty of its situation.

Lower down the creek is thatched **Pandora Inn**, named after the vessel that brought back Captain Bligh after the mutiny on the *Bounty*. **Mylor**, open to the Carrick Roads creek, is excellent for yachting.

Round Trefusis Point, facing Falmouth, is **Flushing**, reputed to have England's mildest climate. It gained its name in the 17th century when Dutch engineers, working on Falmouth's quays, settled here; their influence can still be seen in the tall houses lining the creek-side High Street.

In the 13th century **Penryn** was a seat of religious learning, then it became a major port, which declined as Falmouth grew. The granite and slate-hung buildings now enjoy Conservation Area status.

Above: the old Coinage Hall in Truro now houses a pizzeria and a tearoom.

FALMOUTH

Falmouth ❼ started as a twinkle in Sir Walter Raleigh's eye. In the late 16th century, he decided it would make a good harbour, found Sir John Killigrew, the local lord, very responsive, and the development of the village of Pennycomequick was decided. By 1663 it had become Falmouth.

Falmouth's importance grew with its 1661 Charter. The arrival of the railway in 1863 to serve the new docks heralded

Above: Trelissick Garden, famous for its hydrangeas and camellias, also houses the National Collection of photinias and azaras.

the town's development as a holiday resort. Between the beaches and the station, quiet roads are lined with hotels, guesthouses, villas and gardens, the most lovely of which are **Gyllyngdune Gardens**. Signposted from the seafront, paths lead into a sunken area planted with exotic trees and shrubs.

There are 450 years of military history to be explored at **Pendennis Castle** (English Heritage; Apr–June and Sept daily 10am–5pm, July–Aug daily 10am–6pm, Oct daily 10am–4-pm, Nov–Mar Sat–Sun 10am–4pm; charge). It takes in a Tudor gun deck, underground tunnels and a World War II observation post. Pendennis was built by Henry VIII to protect the estuary from the French – a threat that never materialised. Encircling the headland is **Castle Drive**, which must be the most scenic in the West Country (follow the brown 'Scenic Route' signs).

The quays and the centre

In Arwenack Street, parallel to the sea, the dilapidated **Custom House**, with imposing Greek Doric columns, fronts Custom House Quay, where pub tables stand beside a small fishing harbour. From here, and from **Prince of Wales Pier**, ferries cross to St Mawes and Flushing, and make extended trips to Trelissick and up the River Fal to Malpas and, if the tide's right, to Truro.

Continue along Arwenack Street, lined with shops and restaurants, past the church and up to **The Moor**, Falmouth's municipal heart. Above the library, **Falmouth Art Gallery** (www.falmouthartgallery.com; Mon–Sat 10am–5pm; free) has a permanent display of Victorian and Edwardian paintings and some good temporary

Above: Falmouth's showcase Maritime Museum has a huge collection of boats.

Above: Pendennis Castle has wonderful views over the Fal estuary.

Above: Falmouth was developed after Sir Walter Raleigh rightly decided it would make a good harbour.

exhibitions. Across The Moor, the 111 stone steps of Jacob's Ladder climb the hillside to a pub of the same name. Follow the harbour still further, instead of turning inland, and you will eventually come to the Yacht Marina.

The Maritime Museum

Falmouth is not a wealthy town, but it has undergone a revival with the redeveloped quayside site, **Discovery Quay**. The sophisticated **National Maritime Museum Cornwall** (www.nmmc.co.uk; daily 10am–5pm; charge), dominating the waterfront, is a stunning structure, with a floor-to-ceiling glass viewing gallery. There are lots of hands-on displays, a huge collection of boats of all kinds, and a chance to see traditional boat builders at work – as well as changing exhibitions and fantastic views over the harbour and town from the 95ft (29m) tower.

To the southwest the Helford River almost detaches the Lizard from the rest of Cornwall. From its east coast estuary, this yachting-friendly river cuts through rich woodland and sends inviting creeks through villages. In dramatic contrast, the plateau stretching to Lizard Point, the southernmost part of England, has beauty of a different kind.

GLORIOUS GARDENS

Leaving Falmouth via the popular beach of Swanpool, the road to Mawnan Smith is joined to visit two more wonderful gardens. The first is **Glendurgan Garden** ❽ (NT; mid-Feb–Oct Tue–Sat, also Mon in Aug; charge). Rare, exotic and subtropical plants fill the south-facing slopes of this wooded valley. A fantastic and very photogenic laurel maze, planted in 1833, has been renewed. The views here are great too.

K Poldark Mine

At Wendron, on the B3297, 2 miles (3km) north of Helston, parents with older children can step back in time at the Poldark Mine (www.poldark-mine.co.uk; daily 10am–5.30pm, last tour 4pm, closed Sun Apr–mid-July, Sat Sept–Oct; charge).

The mine was closed in 1820, but its working days and conditions have been re-created alongside workshops and amusements. Winston Graham's popular *Poldark* novels, set in the 19th-century Cornish mining communities, made the name familiar.

Above: Trebah garden is a jungle of delights heading down a ravine to the river.

Above: taking care of rescued seals at the National Seal Sanctuary.

The neighbouring garden, **Trebah** ❾ (www.trebah-garden.co.uk; daily 10am–5pm or dusk; charge), was first planted in the 1840s in a steeply wooded ravine running down to the river. Hydrangeas, rhododendrons and magnolias provide colour, and palms, tree ferns and giant gunnera populate the exotic background.

OYSTERS AND SEALS

A creek is skirted to **Porth Navas**, where the Duchy of Cornwall has an oyster farm, and where the south-going B3291 is joined to reach the tiny village of **Gweek** at the head of the Helford River.

Gweek is home to the **National Seal Sanctuary** (tel: 01326-221 361; www.sealsanctuary.co.uk; daily from 10am, closing times vary; charge), which offers the heartening spectacle of rescued seals and sea lions cared for and returned to the wild after convalescence.

Turn left over the bridge and left through **Mawgan**. Among the monuments in the church are those to the Vyvyans of **Trelowarren** situated in parkland above a long wooded valley.

HELFORD AND COVERACK

Signposted through Manaccan is **Helford ⑩**, which has banished cars to a hilltop park. Daphne du Maurier's **Frenchman's Creek** is at the end of a road to Kestle nearby.

A minor southbound road (joining the B3294 for the last stretch) drops down to pretty little **Coverack ⑪**. Still with a fleet of working boats, the tiny fishing village with thatched, whitewashed cottages is delightful.

Back on the B3293, which climbs to the Goonhilly Downs, standing among the hut circles and burial mounds of prehistory, are the satellite-tracking dishes of **Goonhilly Earth Station ⑫**, once the largest in the world. The Visitor Centre inside was closed in 2010 but the site is now set to undergo major renovation and reopen as a new Science Centre in 2013.

Now take the road that runs through serpentine rock country all the way to Kuggar. The picturesque route descends along a gorge beside a cascading stream.

GETTING TO THE POINT

A great number of the thatched cottages in **Cadgwith ⑬**, at the road's end, downhill from Ruan Minor, are built of the black and green mottled serpentine rock – which brings character to the coved area. Two tiny coves are separated by a rocky viewpoint, the Todden. A pub and pilchard cellars (one now housing the Old Cellars restaurant) complete the picture. The B3083 runs straight down the peninsula to **Lizard**, England's most southerly village.

The **Lizard Lighthouse**, signposted from the village centre, was begun by Sir John Killigrew of Falmouth in 1619, but the present buildings date from 1752.

G Wild Food Walks

Join a guided walk led by specialist Rachel Lambert and learn about the abundance of wild food and how to identify edible plants. The walks take place all year round in the Lizard, West Cornwall, and last 2 to 3 hours. Participants learn about the historical and medicinal uses of local plants. And along with foraging guidelines, you will acquire some tasty new recipes. Tel: 07903 412014; www.wildwalks-southwest.co.uk; charge.

Above: learning to identify what's good to eat and what's not.

Above: wild flowers along the Lizard's cliffs.

KYNANCE COVE

Leaving the B3083, you reach **Kynance Cove** ⓮ on the Lizard's west coast. It is an unforgettable sight at low tide, with the golden sands and the green, red and purple of the serpentine set against the Prussian blue of the sea. **Mullion Cove** has long defied fierce southwesterly gales but climate change and rising sea levels put its future at risk. To the north, before Poldhu Cove, an obelisk on the cliff records the transmission of the first wireless signals across the Atlantic, sent by Guglielmo Marconi in 1901.

Above: there is a roller coaster and funfair at The Flambards Experience.

FLAMBARDS VILLAGE AND HELSTON

Back to the A3083 and, as Helston is approached, you come to a re-created Victorian village in landscaped gardens at Culdrose Manor. This is **The Flambards Experience** ⓯ (tel: 01326-573 404; www.flambards.co.uk; Apr–Oct daily 10.15am–5pm with exceptions, call to check hours; charge). A popular family day out, it includes a funfair with a log flume and roller coaster rides.

Helston ⓰ is a bustling market town that comes alive on 8 May when it celebrates Flora Day. In Old Butter Market, the **Helston Folk Museum** (www.museumsincornwall.org.uk; Mon–Sat 10am–1pm, with exceptions; free) portrays West Cornish life past and present. Water runs down open conduits in Coinagehall Street past the 17th-century **Blue Anchor Inn**, distinguished by its thatched roof and by the quality of the home-brewed beer.

Loe Pool lies just south of Helston, right in the heart of the Penrose Estate. Both are in the care of the National Trust and there is a numerous choice of walking paths through the lovely countryside.

Above: Kynance Cove is a beautiful spot.

HIDDEN TREASURE

Northwest of Helston on the B3302, a left turn leads you to the beautiful Tudor **Godolphin House** (National Trust; garden Feb–mid-Dec 10am–4-pm; charge). This romantic house (closed to the public) and garden have an air of antiquity and peace. The garden boasts an original medieval layout, and is considered to be one of the most important historic gardens in Europe.

Eating Out

Truro

Tabb's

5 Kenwynn Street; tel: 01872-262 110; www.tabbs.co.uk; Tue–Fri lunch and dinner, Sat dinner.

Carefully chosen, seasonal ingredients handled with respect by Chef Nigel Tabb, who keeps the customers happy with his simple dishes. £££

St Mawes

Water's Edge

Idle Rocks Hotel, Harbourside; tel: 01326-270 771; www.idlerocks.co.uk/restaurant.php; daily lunch and dinner.

The menu here has British and French dishes, using local ingredients when possible. Great views; book at weekends and in high season. £££

Mylor

Pandora Inn

Restronguet Creek; tel: 01326-372 678; www.pandorainn.com; daily lunch and dinner.

This slate-floored thatched inn has a great waterside setting. The emphasis is on Cornish produce, especially seafood, and there are cream teas in summer too. ££

Falmouth

Harbourside Restaurant

Harbourside; tel: 01326-312 440; www.greenbank-hotel.co.uk; daily lunch and dinner

This restaurant, set in the Greenbank Hotel – which boasts stunning views – specialises in fish, but meat dishes are also worth a try. You may be tempted by the West Country cheeses. ££–£££

Porthleven (nr Helston)

Kota

The Harbour Head; tel: 01326-562 407; www.kotarestaurant.co.uk; Tue–Sat dinner.

"Kota" is Maori for shellfish, and the restaurant is renowned for its stunning seafood with a light Asian twist. £££

Cornwall Tour 11

Land's End Peninsula and St Ives to St Agnes

This full-day, 65-mile (104km) car tour covers the dramatic tip of the Cornish peninsula before heading inland towards Camborne and Redruth.

PENZANCE

Sunny, south-facing **Penzance ❶** is superbly situated in the embrace of Mount's Bay, where the grandeur of St Michael's Mount provides a focal point. This is one of the warmest places in Britain, with frost and snow nonexistent. The gateway to the Land's End Peninsula, it has air and sea services to the wonderful Isles of Scilly *(see p.108)*.

Highlights

- Penzance
- St Michael's Mount
- Mousehole
- Minack Theatre
- St Ives, the Tate and Barbara Hepworth Museum
- St Agnes

Historical background

Mentioned in the Domesday Book and granted a weekly market by Edward III, Penzance first claimed attention in 1595 when Spanish galleons appeared in the bay and the nearby villages of Paul, Mousehole and Newlyn were sacked and burned. It was also fair game for pirates during the 17th and 18th centuries. Charles II gave it the privilege of coining tin, but only in Victorian times did it assume its present character.

Left: looking out from the Newlyn Art Gallery. **Above**: the flamboyant Egyptian House in Penzance.

K Jubilee Bathing Pool

On a hot summer day, take the kids along to Penzance's Jubilee Bathing Pool (www.jubileepool.co.uk; June–mid-Sept), with separate shallow kiddie pool. Opened in 1935 for the Silver Jubilee of George V, it was one of the best designed lidos of the era and has recently been restored, to much acclaim. Unfortunately, budget cuts make its future uncertain.

Above: Penzance's seawater lido is perfect on a summer's day.

Touring the town

From the east, past the station and inland from the large Wharfside Shopping Centre opposite the harbour, the main thoroughfare, **Market Jew Street**, climbs to the town centre and the grandiose, granite Market House (1836). A statue of Sir Humphry Davy, born nearby in 1778, tempts seagulls. The hand of his statue rests on the miners' safety lamp that bears his name.

There are handsome 18th- and early 19th-century buildings in **Chapel Street**, which runs left from the Market House, many with a ghostly story to tell as Chapel Street is Penzance's oldest street. Today a number of restaurants and art galleries occupy premises here. In Princes Street stands The Exchange (www.newlynartgallery.co.uk; Mon–Sat 10am–5pm, closed Mon in winter; free), a stunning art gallery with an undulating glass facade. The **Egyptian House**, a vividly coloured exercise in Egyptian style, was built in 1838. Further down the street, **St Mary's Church** commands the harbour from a peaceful graveyard.

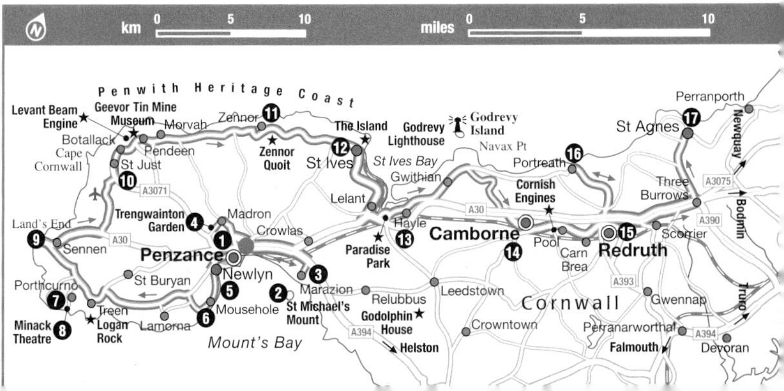

Above: St Michael's Mount has a harbour but can be reached by land at low tide.

Cornish painters

Close by are **Morrab Gardens** where subtropical plants flourish. Wander through and you emerge in Morrab Road, a quiet street lined with guesthouses. At the far end is Penlee Park with a walled memorial garden and the stylishly refurbished **Penlee House Gallery and Museum** (www.penleehouse.org.uk; Mon–Sat, Easter–Sept 10am–5pm, Oct–Easter 10.30am–4.30pm; charge). It is well worth a visit to see many of the works of the Newlyn School painters.

Back on the seafront, a left turn along the broad promenade takes you to the Art Deco **Jubilee Bathing Pool** *(see box p.91)*.

ST MICHAEL'S MOUNT

East of Penzance, the rocky island of **St Michael's Mount** ❷ looms across the bay and, inevitably, comparison is made with the Mont-St-Michel in Normandy. The connection is more than a visual one: England's Edward the Confessor gave the island to the Benedictine monks of St-Michel and, by 1140, they had founded a church there.

The castle (NT; tel: 01736-710507; www.stmichaelsmount.co.uk; Apr–Oct Sun–Fri 10.30am–5/5.30pm, all visits depend on weather conditions; charge) crowns the Mount, which is reached by a cobbled causeway at low tide or by ferry when the tide is high.

Marazion ❸, at the terrestrial end of the causeway, was granted an early charter, in 1257. It became an important market town: the pronunciation of Maghas Yow – Thursday Market – has blurred over the years

Below: Newlyn Art Gallery.

to Marazion. Located on the first floor of the Town Hall (the former fire station) is the **Town Museum** (May–Oct Mon–Fri 10.30am–4.30pm; charge); the back section was once the town gaol and a reconstructed police cell can be viewed.

DETOUR TO TRENGWAINTON GARDEN

From St Michael's Mount, take the A30 west, turn right to Heamoor then to **Trengwainton Garden** ❹ (NT; tel: 01736-363 148; mid-Feb–Oct Mon–Thur 10.30am–5pm; charge). In five intimate walled gardens, semitropical and tender plants not found elsewhere in mainland Britain are grown outdoors. Views over Mount's Bay are shared with **Madron**. Here, in St Maddern's Church, the Trafalgar Banner commemorates news of Nelson's death.

NEWLYN ART

Back in Penzance, leave the town along the promenade. The first building on the left (in New Road) on reaching **Newlyn** ❺ is the large, light space of the **Newlyn Art Gallery** (Mon–Sat 10am–5pm; free). The gallery features the work of artists of regional, national and international importance, and introduces Newlyn as the home of one of Britain's leading art colonies. Here, Stanhope Forbes, Norman Garstin, 'Lamorna' Birch and others set up easels and sent their paintings to the Royal Academy in London. But pretty little Newlyn is not all about art: it has a thriving fishing industry as well.

MOUSEHOLE AND LAMORNA

Downhill from Newlyn Bridge crossroads is **Mousehole** ❻ (pronounced *Mowzel*), the archetypal Cornish fishing

F Ancient Relics

By turning right at Morvah, just past the Geevor Tin Mine on the road to Madron and Penzance, you can see some of the moorland's most interesting relics: Chun Castle, an Iron Age fort; Chun Cromlech, a chamber tomb; Lanyon Quoit; and the oldest – possibly Roman – mine, the Ding Dong. From Zennor, the Neolithic Zennor Quoit, unique in that it covers two tombs, and Giant's Rock, a logan stone on the hill above the church, are both invitingly close.

Above: Lanyon Quoit is thought to have been used for ritual activity.

village. Guests are accommodated in granite cottages in the alleys and courtyards on the hill above.

Continue along the B3315, and after about a mile, turn left at Trewoofe to run alongside a trout stream down the delightful **Lamorna Valley**. A few cottages, an old mill and an inn called The Wink are the setting for a summer idyll. Granite from the quarry was shipped at **Lamorna Cove** to build London's Thames Embankment.

TO MINACK

A mile or so along the B3315 lies a Bronze Age ceremonial site, the Merry Maidens, after which the road soon leads to the village of Treen. From a car park, **Logan Rock**, a huge boulder on the crest of the spectacular headland of Treryn Dinas, can be reached by a footpath.

At nearby **Porthcurno** ❼ is a beautiful beach of golden sand, with just behind it the fascinating **Telegraph Museum** (www.porthcurno.org.uk; daily Apr–Sept 9.30am–5pm, Oct–Mar 10am–3.30pm; charge). The museum is partly housed in World War II fortified tunnels in the cliff.

Above: flag to show lifeguard presence.

Above: snapshot of Mousehole.

Summer brings actors to Porthcurno and the **Minack Theatre** ❽ (www.minack.com; Apr–Sept daily 9.30am–5.30pm, Oct–Mar 10am–4pm; charge; tel: 01736-810 181 for information on afternoon closures on performance days and tickets for performances). This cliff-edge amphitheatre, constructed in the 1930s, was the vision of one woman, the remarkable Rowena Cade.

LAND'S END

The B3315 joins the A30 for **Land's End** ❾, England's most westerly point. Nothing except the Isles of Scilly lies between here and America. The **Land's End Visitor Centre** (tel: 0871-720 0044; www.landsend-landmark.co.uk; daily 10am–closing times vary; free, charge for car park and attractions) is a fun family day out in a complex that embraces a hotel, cafés, interactive and 4 D attractions, birdwatching, speciality shopping and, of course – the famous Land's End signpost.

As you leave on the Penzance road, **Sennen**, England's westernmost village, promises hospitality at the First and Last Inn. Tiny **Sennen Cove**, tucked in under the hill at the western end of Whitesand Bay surfing beach,

Above: spectacular Minack Theatre: the name means 'rocky place' in Cornish.

has pretty thatched cottages and a showcase for modern crafts in the former capstan house.

ST JUST TO ZENNOR

Branching left from the Penzance road, the B3306 soon passes an airfield from which you can fly to the Isles of Scilly *(see p.108)*, and then enters **St Just** ⓾, capital of an industry that died with the fall in the price of tin. With the predominance of granite and slate the town looks rather severe, but it's a friendly place. Cape Cornwall Street leads to **Cape Cornwall**, crowned with a monumental mine chimney.

The coast road traverses an area once mined intensively for tin and copper. July 2006 saw the Cornwall and West Devon Mining Landscape added to the Unesco World Heritage Site list; the Crown's Mine at **Botallack** has the most picturesque of the old mine buildings, with engine houses perched precariously on the cliff. The restored **Levant Beam Engine** (NT; tel: 01736-786 156; mid-Feb–Oct Sun–Fri 11am–5pm) is the oldest working beam engine in Cornwall. Half a mile (1km) along the cliff is **Geevor Tin Mine Museum** (tel: 01736-788 662; www.geevor.com; Apr–Oct Sun–Fri 9am–5pm, Nov–Mar until 4pm, last visit and underground tour an hour before closing; charge).

S Cornish Souvenirs

Apart from model lighthouses and whimsical piskies (Cornish pixies), the main things to buy in Cornwall, as gifts or souvenirs, are food items – gift-wrapped boxes of fudge in an array of flavours are popular, and so is clotted cream, if it isn't going to be transported far. Paintings, drawings or ceramic pieces are also a good choice. There are plenty of galleries and shops to choose from, especially in St Ives, Marazion and Fowey, and some of the work is of high quality.

Above: gifts for sweet friends.

Above: the incomparable harbour at St Ives.

Continuing on the B3306, a church tower signals a chapel, inn and little group of granite dwellings, set among fields strewn with enormous boulders. This is **Zennor** ⓫, where a legendary mermaid lured a chorister beneath the waves after falling in love with his voice *(see also box p.93)*. The fascinating **Wayside Folk Museum** (tel: 01736-796 945; May–Sept daily 10.30am–5-.30pm, Apr and Oct 11am–5pm; charge) traces Zennor's history with its domestic and rural treasures.

ST IVES

The twisting road from Zennor skirts the hills and enters **St Ives** ⓬, the most lively and interesting of all Cornwall's resorts. The road passes Higher Stennack and the **Leach Pottery**, established in 1920 by the late Bernard Leach; some of his work is exhibited here, along with that of other potters.

'The Island'

The most distinguished physical feature of St Ives is 'The Island', which divides the Atlantic surfing beach of Porthmeor from the harbour and from the smaller beach of Porthminster.

Pilchards made St Ives prosperous. Houses were built with fish processing in mind, since salting and packing in barrels for export took place in the cellars below the living quarters. Local industry suffered economic disaster with the disappearance of pilchards, while the miners endured the collapse of the tin market. Survival came from an unexpected quarter: the unique quality of the light and the appeal of the subject matter began to attract artists.

Below: modern art in Tate St Ives.

Above: Barbara Hepworth's garden.

The Tate

Cornwall has its own major art gallery in **Tate St Ives** (tel: 01736-796 226; www.tate.org.uk/stives; Mar–Oct daily 10am–5.20pm, Nov–Feb Tue–Sun 10am–4.20pm; charge). It holds only a small permanent collection of works by St Ives painters – such as Ben Nicholson, Peter Lanyon, Patrick Heron, Sir Terry Frost and Alfred Wallis – instead presenting changing displays from the main Tate Collection, with a focus on works connected with Cornwall, and temporary exhibitions of works by other artists. The building is a delight in itself, as is its position, opposite Porthmeor beach: the view from the restaurant and upper terrace is like a spectacular painting.

An integral part of the Tate is the **Barbara Hepworth Museum** (same hours as the Tate; combined tickets available) in Trewyn Studio on Barnoon Hill. Hepworth's vital spirit is much in evidence in her studio and sculpture garden.

The **St Ives Society of Artists** (founded 1927) shows excellent works at a gallery housed in the light, airy nave of the old Mariners' Church (www.stisa.co.uk; Mar–Dec Mon–Sat 10am–5.30pm, also Sun 2.30–5.30pm in summer), in Norway Square, behind the Sloop Inn. The **Crypt Gallery** also has special exhibitions.

In 1949 a splinter group of modern artists formed the **Penwith Society of Arts**, which exhibits at the **Penwith Galleries** (tel: 01726-795 579; Tue–Sat 10am–1pm, 2.30–5pm), Back Road West. The **St Ives Museum** (www.museumsincornwall.org.uk; Apr–Oct Mon–Fri 10am–5pm, Sat 10am–4pm; charge) covers local history.

The tall granite tower of 15th-century **St Ia** church impresses most from the sea. Inside are barrel roofs, bench-ends, carved columns and Barbara Hepworth's 1954 *Madonna and Child.*

CARBIS BAY AND PARADISE PARK

The A3074 climbs above St Ives' railway station, with panoramic back

St Ives Bay Line

Arriving into St Ives by train is far easier and greener than driving, and the 14-minute journey from St Erth offers spectacular views you cannot see from the road. Opened in 1877, the St Ives Bay Line was the last railway line in Britain to be built to Brunel's broad gauge and is superbly engineered to hug the edge of the cliff around the coast. See www.firstgreatwestern.co.uk for more information.

Above: a train sneaks into St Ives.

Above: the cliffs and beach at pretty little St Agnes.

views over the town *(see box p.97)*, and passes through Carbis Bay where a diversion left leads to the superb Carbis Bay beach.

At **Lelant**, a golf course and church share the sand-hills of the Hayle estuary. Further on, at Hayle, **Paradise Park** (www.paradisepark.org.uk; all year daily from 10am, last admission 5pm, 3pm winter; charge) is the home of the World Parrot Trust, where rare birds and other creatures can be admired.

HAYLE TO GODREVY LIGHTHOUSE

East of St Ives is the heart of Cornwall's former mining industry. **Hayle** ⓭ makes an appropriate introduction because the great beam engines were made here. In **Millpond Gardens**, the foundry's ruins have been laid out as a park.

The road follows the canal through **Copperhouse**, which lost its tin and copper smelting to Swansea. Left at the crossroads beyond, the B3301 passes the *towans* (sand-hills), with splendid views of St Ives across the bay, to reach **Gwithian**.

Just out to sea is the **Godrevy Lighthouse**, the inspiration for Virginia Woolf's 1927 novel *To the Lighthouse*, and beyond is Navax Point (NT), a breeding place for seals. A road forks right from the coast and right again to regain the A30 outside Camborne.

MINES AND ENGINES

At the end of April **Camborne** ⓮ honours Richard Trevithick, 'Father of the Locomotive'. His statue outside the Library on Trevenson Street clutches a model of his steam locomotive, which anticipated Stephenson's *Rocket* by 12 years, but it was for his high-pressure steam-pumping engine that Camborne has most to thank him. At the Library you can find information about the Great Flat Lode Trail and Coast to Coast Trail, part of the **Mineral Tramways Heritage Project**, which have recently been opened up to walkers and cyclists (tel:

Above: remains of a mining past.

01872-222 000). There is little else to see here: Camborne is a town that lost its industry and gained few tourists.

At **Pool**, on the A3047, just outside town, **Cornish Engines** (NT; tel: 01209-315 027; mid-Mar–Oct Sun–Mon, Wed–Fri 11am–5pm, with exceptions; charge) have been lovingly restored and are working smoothly. The first is visible on the right; the other, larger engine and an abandoned mine complex incorporate an audiovisual presentation in the **Industrial Discovery Centre**, tucked behind the supermarket car park to the left. Here too, information leaflets can be collected about the Great Flat Lode Trail and the Coast to Coast Trail.

REDRUTH

Continue east on the A3047 and turn right onto the A393 for **Redruth ⓯**. The Scotsman William Murdock is Redruth's revered celebrity: a prolific inventor, his best-known achievement is gas lighting. His was the first house to be lit by gas, and the light still burns in Cross Street.

PORTREATH

Francis Basset, a local benefactor, created **Portreath ⓰** – reached from Redruth by the B3300 – because there was no suitable port from which to ship ore and import Welsh coal and timber. The harbour, constructed in 1760, was superseded in the early 1800s by a more ambitious one with two inner docks. It is the starting point of the **Coast to Coast Trail**, part of the Mineral Tramways project, and cycles can be hired in Redruth and Bissoe.

ST AGNES

At Scorrier take the A30 towards Newquay, then go left on the B3277 to reach friendly little **St Agnes ⓱**. The village, the cliffs and 600ft (180m), heather-clad St Agnes Beacon all show signs of a mining past. Mining, fishing and folklore take precedence in the **St Agnes Museum** (www.stagnesmuseum.co.uk; Easter–Nov daily 10.30am–5pm; free) in Penwinnick Road, but the prize exhibit is a giant leatherback turtle, washed ashore in 1988.

E Eating Out

Penzance

Abbey Restaurant
Abbey Street; tel: 01736-366 906; www.theabbeyonline.co.uk; Tue–Sat lunch and dinner.
Reliably good and imaginative dishes served in an attractive hotel first-floor dining room with sea views. ££–£££

The Bay
Brighton Hill; tel: 01736-366 890; www.thebaypenzance.co.uk; Sun–Fri 7am–10pm.
Food cooked to perfection all day and sweeping views across the bay. £–££

Mousehole

Old Coastguard Inn
The Parade; tel: 01736-731 222. www.oldcoastguardhotel.co.uk; daily lunch and dinner
Praised for its seafood fresh from the boat and sea views. ££–£££

St Ives

Alba
Old Lifeboat House, Wharf Road; tel: 01736-797 222; www.thealbarestaurant.com; daily dinner only.
Hip, minimalist place housed in a former lifeboat house and renowned for its contemporary menu. ££–£££

Porthminster Beach Café
Porthminster Beach; tel: 01736-795 352; www.porthminstercafe.co.uk; daily lunch and dinner, closed Mon in winter.
Chic, award-winning Mediterranean and Asian seafood restaurant. ££

Cornwall Tour 12

The North Coast Resorts and the Atlantic Highway

Holiday homes, golfers and surfers claim the coastline from Perranporth to Padstow on this 76-mile (122km) tour, while the A39 Atlantic Highway takes a step back at Newquay.

This tour explores a wonderful mix of contrasting landscapes. It could be done in a day but you will get a lot more out of a two-day trip.

Highlights

- Trerice Manor House and Garden
- Padstow
- Prideaux Place
- Port Isaac
- Tintagel Castle
- Boscastle

PERRANPORTH

Perranporth ❶, the first stop on this northern coast, is reached along the winding B3285 from St Agnes. Surfers will find all they need here, and the great stretch of **Perran Sands** is popular with families. The B3285 joins the A3075 at Goonhavern and heads towards Newquay.

NEWQUAY

Newquay ❷ is the biggest and brashest resort on the coast and a magnet for serious surfers. From the south, the road into town crosses the head of the Gannel estuary, and leads to **Fistral Bay**, biggest of the town's three beaches and where the major surfing championships and events are held.

Turning right towards the town centre, you must follow the one-way sys-

Left: Port Isaac, off the Atlantic Highway. Above: surfers in Fistral Bay.

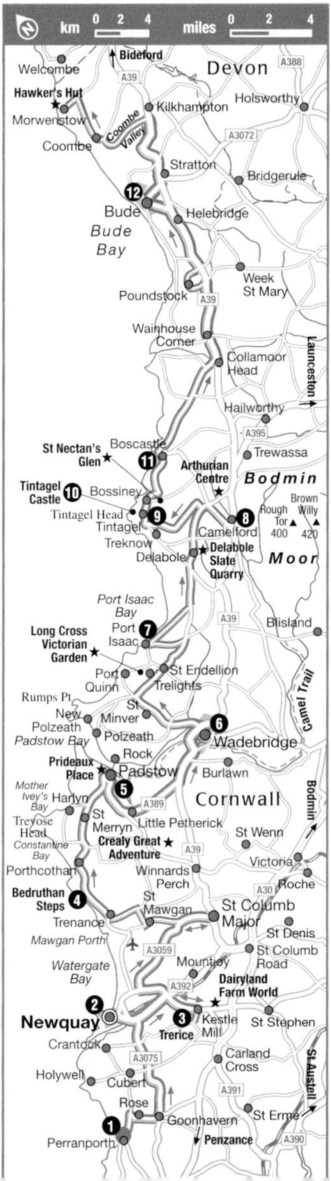

tem. Close to Fore Street is the pretty harbour, and some of the town's oldest houses poised above a sheer cliff face. A road (and a flight of steps) spirals down to the quays, where there's a sandy beach at low tide.

Family entertainment

Newquay is crammed with amusement arcades and fast-food joints, and also has a wealth of family entertainment. The **Blue Reef Aquarium** (www.bluereefaquarium.co.uk; daily from 10am, last admission 4pm; charge) on Towan Promenade is informative and entertaining, and holds fish-feeding demonstrations. **Newquay Zoo** (www.newquayzoo.org.uk; daily, Apr–Oct 9.30am–6pm, Nov–Mar 10am–dusk; charge) at Trenance, off Edgcumbe Avenue, places emphasis on efforts to save animals through captive breeding. On the outskirts of town **Holywell Bay Fun Park** (www.holywellbayfunpark.co.uk; Easter–Oct 10.30am–5.30pm, with exceptions; free, charge for attractions) has over 20 attractions for all ages, from go-carts to blaster boats and pitch and putt.

CHANGE OF PACE

From Newquay take the A392, and turn right on the A3058 to Kestle Mill where signs point to **Trerice** ❸ (NT; house: mid-Feb–Oct daily 11am–5pm, gardens: 10.30am–5pm; charge). Of all Cornwall's country houses, this glorious Elizabethan manor is the most exquisitely furnished and decorated.

Above: the Camel Trail near Padstow *(see also box p.105).*

A return to Kestle Mill and the fringes of Newquay leads to a drive along the A3059, past Newquay Cornwall Airport to **St Columb Major**. It is a peaceful village with a lovely old church, a couple of antique shops and a 16th-century tearoom (erratic opening times) that alone would make the detour worthwhile.

THE VALE OF LANHERNE

Back on the A3059, a first right turn running through woods of the Vale of Lanherne descends to **St Mawgan** and the Falcon Inn. Beyond the wall opposite the church door is **Lanherne**, which has been the seat of the Arundell family since 1231.

COASTAL DIVERSIONS

The hill across the stream and a left-hand turn at the top follows the Vale down to **Mawgan Porth**, where evidence of a 10th-century village coexists with 21st-century holiday accommodation. Northwards, the cliff road climbs to **Bedruthan Steps ❹**, rocks rising from the sand that were, according to legend, the giant Bedruthan's stepping stones. **Porthcothan**, where cliffs with caves and arches are protected by the National Trust, begins a series of bathing beaches: **Treyarnon**, **Constantine**, **Mother Ivey's Bay** and **Harlyn**, all of which are accessible from the B3276.

PADSTOW

Padstow ❺ lies up the estuary beyond the Doom Bar, the sandbank that wrecked many a ship attempting to reach harbour in stormy conditions. The Bar and a silted-up estuary have plagued Padstow for centuries, but it still sustains a small fishing fleet and has an attractive setting.

The church sits below the grounds of **Prideaux Place** (www.prideauxplace.co.uk; Easter, May–Oct Sun–Thur 1.30–5pm, last tour 4pm, grounds: 12.30–5pm; charge), located to the left of the B3276 as you enter Padstow. Home of the Prideaux-Brune family, the richly furnished Elizabethan mansion has often been used as a location for films.

Down on the quay, visitors enjoy

Above: Prideaux Place is a wonderfully restored Elizabethan mansion.

themselves admiring the harbour views and frequenting the small shops, cafés and restaurants that cater to all tastes and pockets – although Rick Stein's impact has raised the culinary tone of the town *(see Eating Out, p.107)*.

On North Quay, ancient **Abbey House** is believed to have been the site of a chapel. From the slipway here, beside the tourist office, the Black Tor ferry runs across the estuary to Rock (daily year-round) and water taxis run throughout the evening until midnight.

In Market Place, **Padstow Museum** (www.padstowmuseum.co.uk; Apr–Oct Mon–Fri 10.30am–4.30pm, Sat 10.30am–1pm; charge) has displays on lifeboats, schooners, shipwrecks, and on the railway that came and went.

The A39 **Atlantic Highway coast** is much loved: romantics flock to Tintagel in search of King Arthur, to Morwenstow in homage to the Reverend Hawker, and to Boscastle, where Thomas Hardy found his first love.

Bad Weather Days

When it's too wet or too cold for the beach, keep children entertained at **Dairyland Farm World** (Summercourt, 4 miles/7km from Newquay; www.dairylandfarmworld.com; Easter–Oct daily 10am–5pm; charge), a country-life museum with pets, ponies and nature trails. Or head to **Crealy Great Adventure** (Tredinnick, nr Wadebridge; www.crealy.co.uk; Apr–mid-Sept daily 10am–5pm, with exceptions; charge) for thrill rides, indoor fun and outdoor adventures.

WADEBRIDGE

From Padstow, the A389 dips to pretty **Little Petherick**, with an ancient stone bridge and church, at the head of the creek. Shortly, a right turn from the bypass descends to **Wadebridge ❻**. A steam railway, the first in Cornwall and second in England, linked Bodmin with Wadebridge in 1834, and in 1899 a branch to Padstow was opened.

Above: Padstow, one of Cornwall's most famous villages, maintains a fishing fleet and prides itself on good restaurants pioneered by Rick Stein.

The tracks have gone, but the **Camel Trail** for walkers and cyclists has replaced them *(see box p.105)*. Wadebridge Station now houses the **John Betjeman Centre** (tel: 01208-81292; Mon–Fri 10am–4pm).

ROCK AND RUMPS

Rock, signposted off the A39 above the bridge, has been connected by ferry to Padstow since the 14th century. Popular with the London rich, it has been dubbed 'Chelsea-on-Sea'. Just beyond Polzeath is **Rumps**, an Iron Age hill fort on a headland.

FROM TRELIGHTS TO PORT ISAAC

Take the B3314 north from Wadebridge and at **Trelights**, en route to St Endellion and behind Long Cross Hotel, is the **Long Cross Victorian Garden** (www.longcrosshotel.co.uk; Apr–Oct daily 9am–6pm; charge). A maze of paths makes every turn in this 2.5-acre (1-hectare) garden of shrubs and herbaceous borders a delight.

From the churchyard at St Endellion on the B3314 a twisting lane drops down to **Port Isaac** ❼. Fish cellars, an inn, a stream and closely packed cottages make it fascinating to explore.

Above: a fishing boat beached beneath the cottages at Port Isaac.

DELABOLE

Over the headland at **Port Gaverne** schooners once loaded slate from Delabole off the beach, and pilchards filled the fish cellars. The continuing road joins the B3314 to enter a village that owes its existence to a hole in the ground – the biggest man-made hole in Britain. **Delabole Slate Quarry** (May–Sept Mon–Fri presentations and tours at 2pm, not BH Mon), down a short road on the right past quarrymen's cottages and chapels, has been worked since medieval times.

Just before the main junction with the A39 turn right for **Camelford** ❽. The long downhill street to the bridge over the River Camel has some attractive buildings. At the entrance to the town is the **North Cornwall Museum and Gallery** (tel: 01840-212 954; Apr–Sept Mon–Sat 10am–5pm; charge). Country trades – those of farmer, cider-maker, carpenter, saddler, cooper, blacksmith – are well represented in re-creating life in moorland parishes over a century ago.

The first right-hand turning from the hill above the Camel bridge allows the closest approach by car to **Rough Tor** (1,312ft/400m), one of Bodmin Moor's two main heights (the other is Brown Willy). Returning to Camelford, a lane on the other side of the A39 crosses a stream at **Slaughterbridge**, the site of King Arthur's last battle and his death. The **Arthurian Centre** (www.arthur-online.co.uk; daily 10am–5pm; charge) has a 'Land of Arthur' exhibition and King Arthur's Stone.

TINTAGEL

Tintagel ❾, suffused with Arthurian legend, is hugely popular so don't go

Above: King Arthur's Tintagel Castle has a dramatic cliff-top setting.

looking for mystical tranquillity. Go late in the afternoon, if you can, when the coach parties will have departed. As you enter the village, **King Arthur's Great Halls** (tel: 01840-770 526; daily 10am–5pm; charge) are straight in front of you, in Fore Street, offering a crash course in the Arthurian Experience – Arthur's story in laser lights, music and sound. The **Old Post Office** (NT; Apr–Sept–Oct daily 11am–5.30pm, Mar and Oct 11am–4pm; charge) is a short way down the road.

Tintagel Castle ❿ (English Heritage; Apr–Oct daily 10am–6pm, Oct until 5pm, Nov–Mar Sat–Sun 10am–4pm; charge) is a short walk from the village. The site, accessible only by a footbridge, is set in a coastline of dramatic black and craggy cliffs, exposed to the fury of the Atlantic. Once the site was occupied by Celts, Romans and Normans. In the 13th century, Henry III's brother Richard, Earl of Cornwall, began a castle which 300 years later had become 'sore wetherbeten and yn ruin'.

SHRINE AND VALLEY

North of Tintagel, beyond Bossiney at Trethevy, the B3263 crosses a stream opposite a free car park. Follow the signs on foot down a path leading to **St Nectan's Glen**, with a 60ft (18m) waterfall and a shrine called St Nectan's Kieve (www.st-nectansglen.

G The Camel Trail

The Camel Trail covers 18 miles (28km), following the course of the old LSWR railway line, between Padstow and Blisland. Bikes can be hired from Bridge Bike Hire near the Old Bridge in Wadebridge (tel: 01208-813 050). You can, of course, bring your own bike, and join the trail at various points.

Above: railway bridge for cyclists.

co.uk; daily Apr–Oct 9am–5pm, Nov–Mar 10.30am–3pm; charge). Many people regard the shrine as a sacred site.

You reach **Boscastle** ⓫ by way of Paradise, the hilltop area around the Napoleon Inn, and descend, on the right, the steep village street lined with ancient, whitewashed cottages. From the main car park a path follows the beautiful Valency Valley to the church of **St Juliot**, where, in 1870, young Thomas Hardy, on an architectural mission to restore the local church, met his first wife, Emma, sister-in-law of the rector. The fascinating **Museum of Witchcraft** (www.museumofwitchcraft.com; tel: 01840-250 111; Apr–Oct Mon–Sat 10.30am–6pm, Sun 11.30am–6pm; charge) showcases quirky witchcraft artefacts. In 2002 Boscastle suffered one of the worst floods in Britain's history, though no lives were lost, and buildings have since been restored.

F Hawker's Legacy

From 1834 to 1875, the Rev Robert Hawker was parson of St John's church in Morwenstow. An eccentric but compassionate man, he gave Christian burial to sailors from ships wrecked below the treacherous cliffs. In the churchyard is the figurehead of the *Caledonia*, the sailing ship from Arbroath in Scotland whose crew found a resting place here in 1842. Hawker also revived a pagan custom when he gave an autumn thanksgiving service in his church in 1843: Harvest Festival, as it became known, is now so much a part of church ritual that it is easy to forget that it was Hawker's creation.

Above: Rev Hawker (1803–75), poet and the man behind Harvest Festival.

BUDE

From Boscastle, the B3263 joins the A39 for **Bude** ⓬. The river struggles through the sand to the Haven, dividing the bathers and surfers of Summerleaze and Crooklets beaches, and the golfers and tennis players on the cliffs above, from the castle in the dunes and the canal on the south side. **Bude Canal**, begun in 1823 with the intention of linking the Bristol and English channels, reached no further than Launceston, and the arrival of the railway in the 1890s ended its working life. Only a short length of water remains.

Bude Canal's history is told in the **Bude Heritage Centre** (Easter–Oct daily 11am–5pm; charge), which is housed in a castle surrounded by landscaped grounds. The small castle was built as a seaside residence in 1850 by Sir Goldsworthy Gurney, inventor of one of the earliest steam locomotives and of the Bude Light, which was used to illuminate the House of Commons.

THE VICAR OF MORWENSTOW

The A39 continues towards the Devon border. Two diversions can be made en route: first to the beautiful **Coombe Valley**; second to **Morwenstow**, Cornwall's northernmost point. This was the parish of eccentric 19th-century vicar, Robert Hawker *(see box, left)*. Near the top of the treacherous cliffs

Above: typical whitewashed cottage inn in Boscastle.

is **Hawker's Hut**, the timber-framed shack where he watched out for ships in danger, mourned his wife and sought inspiration for his poetry. It is under the protection of the National Trust and must be its smallest property.

Eating Out

Newquay

Beach Hut Bistro
Watergate Bay; tel: 01637-860 877; www.watergatebay.co.uk/thebeachhut.htm; daily breakfast, lunch and dinner.
This cheerful place is an extremely popular place to hang out. Enjoy brilliant breakfasts, lazy lunches, sundowner drinks and great fish dishes, all with stunning views. Best to book. £–££

Fifteen Cornwall
Watergate Bay; tel: 01637-861 000; www.fifteencornwall.co.uk; daily breakfast, lunch and dinner.
Jamie Oliver's beachfront, Italian-inspired venture offers excellent fresh fish and organic produce from local farmers, fishermen and growers. £££

New Harbour Restaurant
Old Fishing Harbour (off South Quay Hill); tel: 01637-874 062; www.finns2go.com; daily lunch and dinner.
This place serves up innovative fish and seafood combinations with a speciality in lobster, but non-fish and vegetarian options are plentiful. ££–£££

Padstow

Rick Stein's Café
8 Middle Street, tel: 01841-532 700. www.rickstein.com; all day.
This is a less expensive version of Stein's famous St Petroc's Bistro, in a pleasant wood-panelled restaurant. Booking advisable for dinner. ££

The Seafood Restaurant
Riverside; tel: 01841-532 700; www.rickstein.com; daily lunch and dinner.
This pleasant, relaxed Rick Stein haven has a central seafood bar where you can watch his chefs at work. The set-price lunch menu is very good. £££

St Petroc's Bistro
4 New Street; tel: 01841-532 700; www.rickstein.com; daily lunch, Thur–Sun dinner.
Enjoy bistro classics such as Bayonne Ham with Celeriac Remoulade, Moules Marinières, and Steak Frites in Stein's own small hotel. £££

Bude

Life's a Beach
Summerleaze Beach; tel: 01288-355 222; www.lifesabeach.info; daily breakfast, lunch and dinner.
Overlooking the beach and with fabulous seafood at reasonable prices. A wide-ranging menu reflects the creativity of the young talented chefs. £–££.

Tour 13

The Isles of Scilly

With such clear air, vivid blue water and year-round warmth, the Isles of Scilly seem far from Britain. Prepare to island-hop and don't be in a rush.

This small cluster of islands 28 miles (45km) southwest of Land's End comprises five inhabited islands (pop. 2,200) and over 100 smaller islands. The islands are tiny – the largest, St Mary's, is barely 3 miles (5km) at its widest point. A mild climate means tropical plants and bulbs thrive; together with tourism these form the mainstay of the economy, although the flower industry is declining. The islands can be equally magical in bad weather. In winter they face the full force of the Atlantic. For details of how to get here, *see p.121*.

Highlights

- Isles of Scilly Museum
- Tresco Abbey Gardens
- Bryher
- St Agnes
- St Martin's

MYTH AND REALITY

Steeped in myth and legend, the islands have been associated with the Arthurian Lyonesse, the Atlantis of the Greeks and the Cassiterides (tin islands) of the Phoenicians. What is certain is that they have been inhabited for at least 4,000 years, as countless Bronze Age burial mounds testify.

For much of their history, the islanders had to scratch a living from anything the sea had to offer, including shipwrecks. Prosperity only arrived in 1834 when Augustus Smith obtained the lease of the islands. He made social reforms and encouraged shipbuilding.

Left: St Mary's beach. **Above**: World Pilot Gig Championship, Hugh Town.

Ⓕ Scilly Facts

- Owing to the Scillonian people's assistance when the German ocean liner Schiller was shipwrecked nearby in 1875, orders were given during the two World Wars to spare the islands from German attack.
- St Mary's is the final resting place of former British prime minister Harold Wilson, who was very fond of the islands.
- The gigs in the Isles of Scilly Museum can be seen in action by summer visitors; they race between the Tresco Channel and St Mary's every Wednesday and Friday evening in the gig races.

ST MARY'S

Shipyards once occupied the beach adjacent to the quayside at **St Mary's**, the first port of call for visitors arriving by sea. It is only a short walk into the Scillies' main town, **Hugh Town**, which straddles the island at its narrowest point. You could visit the **Mermaid** pub before continuing up the road on the right, through the **Garrison Gate** to **Star Castle**. Now a hotel, the castle was built in 1593 as protection against pirates and possible invasion by the Spanish. In 1646, during the Civil War, the castle was a refuge for the Prince of Wales (Charles II) and his retinue after their defeat at Bodmin.

ISLES OF SCILLY MUSEUM

Continue through Hugh Town into Church Street, where the **Isles of Scilly Museum** ❶ (Mon–Sat, Apr–Sept 10am–4.30pm, Nov–Feb 10am–noon; charge) offers an interesting insight into life on the islands. Exhibits range from Bronze and Iron Age artefacts to remnants of shipwrecks. The museum's centrepiece is a restored pilot boat (gig). A natural history section highlights species that live here for at least part of the year. The puffin and the Atlantic seal are popular residents of the Western Rocks.

St Mary's has some magnificent coastline, nowhere more than at **Penninis Head** on the south coast. There is also much evidence of ancient history on the island, including **Bant's Carn Burial Chamber**.

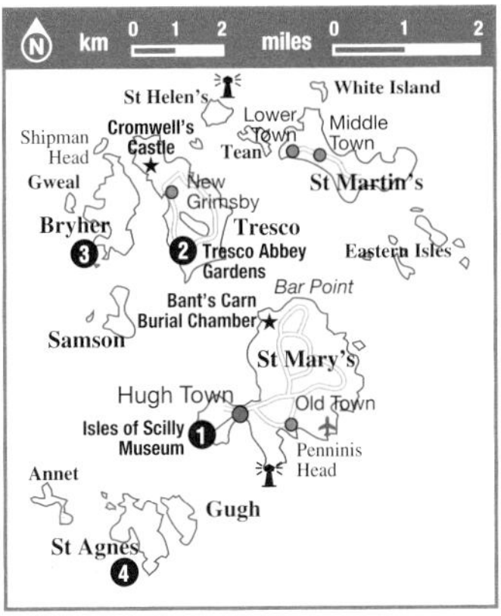

TRESCO

Depending on the tide, visitors to the paradise island of **Tresco** usually arrive at **New Grimsby** harbour. A long promenade leads around the harbour, where the road turns left uphill to Old Grimsby. Most visitors continue straight on, following signs to **Tresco Abbey Gardens** ❷ (www.tresco.co.uk; all year daily 9.30am–4pm; charge). Laid out in the 19th century by Augustus Smith, the gardens contain rare plants from 80 countries, ranging from Brazil to New Zealand and Burma to South Africa, many brought back by ships' captains. In the gardens is the **Figurehead Valhalla**, a museum of figureheads culled from shipwrecks.

The southern end of Tresco is flanked by a series of beautiful, empty beaches. Continue along the east coast past Pentle Bay and the Old Blockhouse to **Old Grimsby**, from where it is possible to explore the rugged northern end of the island, whose features include **Pipers' Hole**, a cave with a small underground lake. On the west coast the most distinctive man-made feature is the tower of **Cromwell's Castle**, built on the promontory beneath the older King Charles' Castle in 1651.

Above: Cromwell's Castle on Tresco, built beneath King Charles' Castle.

BRYHER

Just opposite Tresco is **Bryher** ❸, the smallest of the five inhabited islands, with a population of around 80. The settled part of the island starts at the **church** by the main quay and winds uphill, dropping down to the coast once more at the **Fraggle Rock Café** *(see Eating Out, p.111)*. A path leads up to the northern tip, offering beautiful walks over the downs. The rocky headland of **Shipman Head** is separated from the island by a narrow cleft; so having visited **Hell Bay**, which even on a day of moderate swell offers spectacular views of the sea lashing against the rocks, walkers can continue down the west coast.

The most beautiful feature at the island's southern end, **Rushy Bay** overlooks uninhabited **Samson** island. Behind the bay is **Samson Hill**, from which there are superb views.

ST AGNES AND ST MARTIN'S

St Agnes ❹ is the most southwesterly community in the whole of the British Isles. Principal industries are fishing and flower growing. At low

Above: Tresco is dotted with almost deserted white-sand beaches.

tide you can walk across a sandbar to the small island of **Gugh**. Near the main jetty is the Turk's Head, renowned for good food and fine views. In the centre of the island, and visible from afar, is a disused, 17th-century, coal-burning lighthouse. An even more striking feature, the red-and-white-striped Daymark dominates the easternmost inhabited island of **St Martin's**, popular for its magnificent beaches.

E Eating Out

St Mary's

Bell Rock Hotel Restaurant
Church Street; tel: 01720-422 575; www.bellrockhotel.co.uk; daily dinner only.
A cosy restaurant using local produce whenever possible, such as free-range Scillonian eggs, Cornish cheeses and award-winning sausages. ££

Bishop and Wolf
Hugh Town; tel: 01720-422 771; all day, food served noon–2pm, 6–8pm
Good pub food and drink in one of the oldest buildings in town. £

Juliet's Garden
Seaways Flower Farm, Portloo Beach; tel: 01720-422 228; http://julietsgardenrestaurant.co.uk; daily lunch and dinner.
Views from the terrace over the harbour are breathtaking and the food is extraordinary (especially the huge crab salad). A converted barn loft provides the indoor seating. £–££.

Bryher

Fraggle Rock Café
tel: 01720-422 222; Tue–Sun lunch and dinner, reduced hours in winter.
England's most westerly pub, Fraggle Rock provides drinks, snacks (including the famous crab double-decker sandwich) and evening meals. £

St Martin's

Tean Restaurant
St Martin's Hotel, Lower Town; tel: 01720-422 092; www.stmartinshotel.co.uk; daily breakfast and dinner.
This fine-dining restaurant boasts awesome views of the sunsets over the Round Island Lighthouse. ££–£££

RIP CURL
ACT
SURFBOARDS

Travel Tips

Active Pursuits

The great outdoors of Devon and Cornwall are ideal for all kinds of outdoor activities. Choose from walking, cycling, golf, riding, fishing and all manner of water sports, including, of course, surfing.

WALKING

Devon's most famous long-distance routes are the Templer Way, Two Moors Way, Tarka Trail, and the South West Coast Path. Both moors have guided walks, organised by the National Parks themselves and usually with a ranger as guide. Check out www.visitdevon.co.uk or www.devon.gov.uk for detailed information.

Also worth it if you are in Devon in the autumn is the South Devon Walking Festival (www.southdevonwalkingfestival.co.uk), with a programme of nearly 50 walks to enjoy throughout the South Devon area. Themes include wildlife, history and heritage, wild food, coastal farming and geology.

In Cornwall the South West Coast Path, the Camel Trail and Cardinham Woods all offer great walking. For information on the South West Path, visit www.swcp.org.uk. For information on the 2004 'Right to Roam' legislation, check www.ramblers.org.uk. Other useful sites include www.parow.org.uk; www.aonb.org.uk; www.countrywalks.com and www.cornwallwildlifetrust.org.uk.

CYCLING

Some walks have also been designated **cycleways**, but mountain bikers are asked to stick to the agreed routes. Bikes can be hired throughout the counties. For useful information on the major routes and details of cycle hire opportunities, check out www.visitdevon.co.uk; www.cycledevon.info and www.visitcornwall.com.

Cornish Cycle Tours (www.cornish

cycletours.co.uk) offers cycling holidays in Cornwall's most scenic areas, staying at charming places. For the Camel Trail, call Bridge Bike Hire, tel: 01208-81305; or Padstow Cycle Hire, tel: 01841-533 533. For general information, check www.nationalcyclenetwork.org.uk.

FISHING

In Devon **game fishing** for trout is popular on the fringes of both moors. Local hotels usually have fishing rights, or can make arrangements for guests. The Exe, the Torridge, the Taw, the Tamar and the Dart are salmon rivers. Local hotels such as the Rising Sun at Umberleigh are popular with salmon fishermen. **Sea-fishing** in the region can be fruitful, but less so from the shore than from a boat. For general information about fishing in the South West see www.gethooked.co.uk.

GOLF

Golf links are often set in superb coastal sites. In Devon alone there are over fifty courses, including Torquay, Dartmouth, Okehampton and Ilfracombe. In Cornwall St Enedoc Golf Club, Rock (tel: 01208-83216; www.st-endoc.co.uk), has two courses, as does St Mellion Golf Club, Saltash (tel: 01579-351 351; www.st-mellion.co.uk), where one is designed by Jack Nicklaus. For more details, visit: www.golfindevon.co.uk and www.golfincornwall.co.uk.

HORSE RIDING

Horse riding is popular on both moors in Devon. On Exmoor try Burrowhayes Farm (tel: 01643 862 463; www.burrowhayes.co.uk) or Keypitts,

Preceding Pages: surfers at Fistral Bay, Newquay. **Left**: pony trekking in Exmoor National Park. **Below**: cycling in Dartmoor National Park.

Birdwatching

The Fal Estuary, Gerrans Bay and the surrounding coastline are ideal spots for birdwatching. A huge number of sea birds, divers, waders and sea ducks are either resident here or regular winter visitors. Most of this coastline is managed by the National Trust and there are footpaths along much of its length. For more details, contact the **Cornwall Bird Watching and Preservation Society** (www.cbwps.org.uk) or the **Cornwall Wildlife Trust** (tel: 01872-273 939; www.cornwallwildlifetrust.org.uk). Also check out www.scilly-birding.co.uk.

Above: the Isles of Scilly teem with birdlife, such as oystercatchers.

(also quadbiking; tel: 01271-862 247, www.keypitts.com). On Dartmoor try Eastlake (tel: 01837-52513; www.eastlakeridingstables.co.uk). In Cornwall, establishments offering riding and trekking for all ages and abilities include: Denby Riding Stables, Nanstallon, nr Bodmin, tel: 01208-72013; Penhalwyn Trekking Centre and School, Goon Mine Mellyn, Halsetown, St Ives, tel: 01736-796 461; Tresallyn Riding Stables, Padstow, tel: 01840-520 454.

WATER SPORTS

There is excellent **white-water canoeing** on the River Dart, and to a lesser extent the Barle and the Exe in Devon. A couple of the river estuaries – notably the Dart and the creek at Salcombe – have **summer canoeing**. To hire kayaks try Kayaks and Paddles Ltd., Plymouth, tel: 01752-892 672, no experience necessary. **Sea-canoeing** takes place along the south coast at Dartmouth and Salcombe, where craft can be hired.

Sailing thrives in the creeks of South Devon, particularly around Salcombe. Here the Island Cruising Club (tel: 01548-531 176; www.icc-salcombe.co.uk) organises learn-to-sail breaks based on its converted Mersey ferry. In Cornwall the Fal and Camel estuaries offer some fine sailing. Details from sailing clubs at Falmouth (tel: 01326-211 311), Fowey (tel: 01726-832 335), Flushing, Helford River (tel: 01326-231 460), Looe (tel: 01503-262 559), and St Mary's, Isles of Scilly (tel: 01720-422 060). South West Lakes Trust also runs water-sports centres: www.swlakestrust.org.uk.

Surfing

Cornwall's exhilarating Atlantic coast offers some of the best surfing in the country at Fistral Bay, Lusty Glaze and Watergate Bay, Newquay, and Porthmeor Beach, St Ives; but Bude, St Agnes and Perranporth are also strong contenders. In all these places you can hire or buy equipment, take lessons, and be assured of qualified instructors and lifeguards. All the

Family Fun Activities

The Manor House Hotel (www.manorhousehotel.com) near Okehampton is a home from home with the bonus of family fun activities. Kids can enjoy an indoor swimming pool, fun pool with waterslides, tennis and badminton, 10-pin bowling, pedal karts, indoor adventure playhouse, Gamezone, and lots more. With golf and craft lessons also on the menu, there's plenty for grownups too.

Above: surfers racing to the waves at Woolacombe beach.

Above: sailing is a great way to explore craggy coves and inlets.

schools listed below have the British Surfing Association seal of approval.

In Newquay, the Watergate Bay Surf School (on the beach, tel: 01637-860 543; www.watergatebay.co.uk) offers tuition by the half or full day, with all-in prices for lessons, equipment and accommodation if required. Also in Newquay, the Escape Surf School (35 Fore Street, tel: 01637-805 624; www.escapesurfschool.co.uk) has similar deals. Many shops in town hire or sell equipment.

In St Ives, the St Ives Surf School (tel: 01736-793 938; www.stivessurfschool.com) offers tuition and equipment hire, as does Surf's Up Surf School (tel: 01208-862 003; www.surfsupsurfschool.com) at Polzeath nearer Bude. In Widemouth Bay, Bude, the environmentally aware Outdoor Adventure Multi-Activity and Surf School (tel: 01288-362 900, www.outdooradventure.co.uk) specialises in yachting and canoeing as well as surfing, and offers accommodation. In Perranporth, the Blue Wings Surf School (tel: 01637-874 445) gives lessons.

For up-to-the-minute tide and wind conditions and the best surfing spots, check www.bbc.co.uk/cornwall/surfing or www.magicseaweed.com. For general surfing information, check www.cornwalls.co.uk/surfing or www.surfing-cornwall.com.

Below: canoes and kayaks are readily available to rent at most coastal resorts and popular beaches.

Themed Holidays

A growing interest in specialist holidays has led to several organisations offering breaks with a theme. Choose from painting, conservation work, yoga, interior design, foraging and cooking, spa sessions and more.

VOLUNTEERING

If you care passionately about the conservation of Devon and Cornwall's historic houses, gardens, coast and countryside, the National Trust offer working holidays for volunteers. Jobs include welcoming visitors, stewarding, gardening, environmental and artefact conservation. Help is needed too for the day-to-day running of buildings and open spaces, in offices and with special events.

Groundwork South West also offers volunteering opportunities arranged so that participants can work different days of the week and weekends too. And Responsible Travel offers short breaks in Cornwall assisting with coastal conservation.

Below: volunteers repairing a dry-stone wall on a National Trust Working Holiday on Exmoor, Devon.

CONSERVATION

If you opt for a Helpful Holidays cottage break you can relax and enjoy your holiday knowing that they operate a Green Cottage Scheme, which encourages their home owners to think sustainability. At Cornwall Holiday Cottage Kingsmill in the Tamar Valley, Valerie Taplin has created a wild-flower meadow and established a large freshwater lake.

'The cottage is on the banks of the tidal creek,' reveals Valerie, 'so guests can spot buzzards, owls, ducks, herons, swans, little egret, kingfishers, badgers and deer.'

PAINTING

If painting is your thing, consider Newlyn where Rose Farm Studios offers painting holidays. Experienced tutor Tim Hall supervises courses to help budding artists tackle a new medium, improve their skills or try painting outside. All materials are provided and class sizes are restricted, and artist in residence Henrietta Graham is available for tea and talk about painting matters. Accommodation is also available at the Rose Farm.

Still on an artistic theme, the Hamptons Hotel in Ilfracombe offers interior design courses by owner Janine Powell who in a previous life taught the subject at university level. Participants can choose from one called 'fall in love with your house again', 'preparing your home for sale' or "be your own Interior designer".

Another specialist course is available for people thinking of setting up their own hotel, or hoteliers and B&B owners who want to improve their property. All packages include accommodation, materials and meals.

FORAGING AND COOKING

Do you know your wood sorrel from your Cornish round leaf mint, or how about wild borage from pennywort?

Fowey's Old Quay House Hotel has teamed up with the Wild Food School in Lostwithiel to introduce a quirky but popular package of accommodation and wild food foraging. If you've never done this before then you'll be amazed at just how much fun it can be learning about wild ingredients and gathering a selection for the pot: Thai hedge garlic fish curry, lentil and ramsons soup, borage sambal and rice, sloe gin, even dandelion coffee.

Foraging for wild food is the complete counterculture to supermarket homogeneity and uses new skills to find seasonal, nutritionally rich and interesting ingredients for free. It is a totally immersive experience exploring sheltered stretches of the River Fowey, nearby country lanes and the forest floor of our local deciduous and evergreen woodlands. As the seasons change so too does the wealth and availability of edible wild plants.

Trips are led by food historian and wild food aficionado Marcus Harrison. Head chef Ben Bass then takes participants into his kitchen for some impromptu cooking of wild greens such as sweet violet leaves, ground ivy and wild strawberry to prepare nutty-flavoured acorn tagliatelle, or Thai-style oak forest curry. Bon appétit!

YOGA AND SPA HOLIDAYS

Yoga holidays, spa breaks and meditation holidays can be booked at several venues around Cornwall. Classes are led by a qualified British Wheel of Yoga teacher and in many cases packages include spa treatments. Choose from sites at Helford River, Crantock, Newquay and Polzeath. If you are a spa aficionado, top places include St Moritz Spa Hotel in Polzeath, located above Daymer bay in Trebetherick, and The Bay Hotel and Fistral Spa in Newquay. The Budock Vean Hotel spa has a heated indoor pool, log fires and over 60 acres (24 hectares) of parkland along with all the pampering you can handle.

For Thalgo treatments using the riches of the sea, check out Newquay's Retallack Resort and Spa at St Columb. And at Falmouth's St Michael's Spa Hotel fitness fans can pump iron at a well-equipped fitness suite, try a body wrap, swim, indulge in a massage and facial or enjoy a complete detox.

Below: the stunning scenery begs to be immortalised on canvas.

ADVENTURE SPORTS

If you fancy getting your adrenalin going with an exciting new activity, for the very brave (or foolhardy), Coasteering Newquay offers action-packed holidays that include accommodation, breakfast, instruction and equipment. In this madcap sport, you navigate the coast by jumping off cliffs, swimming into tiny caves and crossing white-water currents.

For those who prefer to stay closer to the ground, or the water, they also offer surfing, kayaking, quad biking, kite buggying and lots more at which to try your hand.

Above: Devon is the place for surfing holidays.

USEFUL WEBSITES

www.nationaltrust.org.uk
www.southwest.groundwork.org.uk
www.responsibletravel.com
www.helpfulholidays.com
www.kingsmillcornwall.co.uk
www.cornwallpaintingholidays.co.uk
www.thehamptonshotel.com
www.theoldquayhouse.com
www.stmoritzhotel.co.uk
www.newquay-hotels.co.uk
www.budockvean.co.uk
www.retallackresort.co.uk
www.stmichaelshotel.co.uk
www.geniusloci.co.uk (for yoga, spa, music, photography, painting and many more holidays in Cornwall)
www.coasteeringnewquay.com

Above: some Tourist Information Centres organise volunteering programmes.

Practical Information

GETTING THERE

Devon and Cornwall are large counties with few major transport arteries. Public transport is widespread, but so is the population, so don't expect to get anywhere in a hurry. Schedules tend to vary according to local market days and to seasons.

By road

Most car travellers arrive in Devon via the M5 motorway, which is fed by the M4 from London (roughly 200 miles/ 320km) and the M6 from the north.

The nearest motorway to Cornwall, the M5 (connections with the M4 at Bristol and the M6, at Birmingham), ends at Exeter, from where the main routes into Cornwall are the A30 to Penzance and the A38 to Bodmin via Plymouth. North Cornwall is served by the Atlantic Highway (A39).

City-centre parking in Devon and Cornwall is quite good, with several multistorey car parks. Most other locations have pay-and-display car parks, not cheap. Parking is often a problem in summer. Park and Ride rail schemes are run in high season at Liskeard (for Looe), St Austell (for the Eden Project) and Lelant Saltings (for St Ives).

Above: if you are driving on the more remote roads of both counties, look out for grazing livestock!

By coach

National Express has regular services into the region. The journey time London–Penzance is about 8.5 hours. For further information: www.traveline.info or tel: 0871-200 2233.

By train

Exeter is served by fast trains (less than 3 hours) from Paddington. An alternative London slower service (Regional Railways) runs from Waterloo.

Fast trains, operated by First Great Western, run from London Paddington to various towns in the West. Direct journey time London–Penzance is about 6 hours; www.firstgreatwestern.co.uk. Virgin Trains run from central and northern England plus Scotland; www.virgintrains.co.uk.

For all train information, contact National Rail Enquiries, tel: 0845-748 4950; www.nationalrail.co.uk or visit www.thetrainline.com.

By air

Exeter and Newquay have airports

Exeter airport information, tel: 01392-367 433; www.exeterairport.co.uk; Plymouth, tel: 01752-204 090; www.plymouthairport.com; Newquay Airport tel: 01637-860 600; www.newquaycornwallairport.com.

To the Isles of Scilly

British International Helicopters operates chopper services between Penzance and the islands, tel: 01736-363 871; www.islesofscillyhelicopter.com. The Isles of Scilly Steamship Group offers fixed-wing flights and boat services, tel: 01736-362 009; www.chycor.co.uk/tourism/issc/steamship.htm. Or book air and ferry services online at www.islesofscilly-travel.co.uk.

GETTING AROUND

By car

Many of the country lanes have narrow stretches and there are plenty of steep hills. Allow double time for all car journeys, and don't try to hurry. The region's roads were not built for speed, and there's likely to be a tractor, herd of cows, or caravan somewhere just ahead.

In general, it is always good to know the market days of your local town, because these greatly affect the amount of traffic making its way to the centre. To steer clear of local traffic congestion, tune into BBC Radio Cornwall for regular bulletins on traffic.

Car rental

Major companies have offices in Exeter, Plymouth and Newquay.

Budget Exeter, tel: 01392-422 095
Avis Plymouth, tel: 0844 544 6090
Thrifty Plymouth, tel: 01752-207 207
Europcar Newquay, tel: 01637-860 337.

By train

From Exeter (St Davids) regional connections go to Barnstaple and Exmouth, and from Newton Abbot to Paignton. From Plymouth, a service runs up the Tamar Valley all the way to Gunnislake.

Regional Railways operate a service between Plymouth and Penzance via Liskeard and Truro, with lines heading off to Gunnislake, Looe, Newquay, Falmouth and St Ives. For more information on how to get around without a car, visit www.carfreedaysout.com.

Below: train rides can be eventful along the coast.

By bus

The local bus network is extensive and services are fairly reliable. Visit www.travelinesw.com, and more details are available from First Devon and Cornwall Bus companies (www.firstgroup.com/ukbus). Other services are run by Western Greyhound (tel: 01637-871 871; www.western-greyhound.com) and Stagecoach South West (tel: 01392-437 711; www.stagecoachbus.com).

By bike

Cyclists can travel several car-free routes including the Tarka Trail and Cornwall's Clay Trail. The Surf and Cycle Bus runs between Barnstaple and Woolacombe via Croyde, with the complete lower floor converted to allow surfboard and cycle storage.

By taxi

For short distances around cities, taxis are inexpensive.
Jay Cars, Exeter, tel: 01392-217 000
Silverline Taxis, Plymouth, tel: 01752-242 424
A2B Taxis, Newquay, tel: 01637-875 555
Roger Care Taxis, Penzance, tel: 01736-367 433.

GREEN TRANSPORT

For low-impact travel use public transport. First Devon and Cornwall has introduced Drive Green technology on its buses. And there are plans to introduce greener bi-mode trains (running on both diesel and electricity) on slower rail services.

FACTS FOR THE VISITOR

Disabled travellers

For suitable accommodation, try www.radar.org.uk or call RADAR, tel: 0207-250 3222.

Other useful sites to visit include: www.disabledholidaydirectory.co.uk; www.accessiblecountryside.org.uk; www.goodaccessguide.co.uk; www.tourismforall.org.

Above: road signs in Bickleigh, mid-Devon.

Emergencies

For emergency ambulance, fire or police dial 999. The Royal Cornwall Hospital, Treliske, Truro TR1 3LJ, tel: 01872-250 000 has a full Accident and Emergency (A&E) Department.

Opening hours

Most shops open from 9am to 5.30pm; supermarkets usually stay open later, and some open on Sunday. Post offices open Monday–Friday 9am to 5.30pm, and usually until noon on Saturday. There are plenty of late-night garages.

Tourist information

For information on Devon check out www.visitdevon.co.uk. For Tor Bay (Torquay, Paignton and Brixham), www.englishriviera.co.uk and for Mid and North Devon, www.northdevon.com. For Lundy Island, www.lundyisland.co.uk.

For information on Cornwall, check www.visitcornwall.com. For Scilly, www.simplyscilly.co.uk.

Accommodation

Devon and Cornwall offer just about every type of accommodation to suit your needs and pocket. Booking is essential during high summer, but not always at other times.

Farm stays are increasingly popular, as are self-catering cottages. Holiday camps, caravan sites and camping facilities are widespread, particularly in coastal areas. To tipi or not to tipi is the perennial camping question. Tipis usually come kitted out with bed rugs, rolls, lanterns and mini cooker so you can play cowboys and Indians in total comfort.

B&B, CAMPING AND CARAVANNING WITH THE NATIONAL TRUST

More than 80 tenants of National Trust properties offer bed-and-breakfast accommodation. Most of it is fairly inexpensive and invariably the properties are attractive ones, set in rural areas. Sleeping in the great outdoors can be lots of fun too. The NT campsite at Highertown Farm has fine views of the southeast Cornwall coast and is situated near a secluded beach. Dunscombe Manor Caravan Park is located in 15 acres (almost 7 hectares) of unspoilt countryside. Lundy Island also has NT camping and caravanning.

There are several YHA youth hostels in the region, including on Dartmoor and Exmoor, and at Exeter, Salcombe, Plymouth, the Lizard, Penzance and Boscastle. Camping barns, or 'stone tents', are owned by individual farmers, but co-ordinated by the YHA. Barns vary, but showers and cooking facilities are standard. Many are located on long-distance footpaths and cycle trails.

Above: sumptuous room at the Carlyon Bay Hotel, perched high above St Austell Bay.

HOTELS

Price categories are for a double room with breakfast in mid-summer:

£££	over £180
££	£100–£180
£	under £100

Bigbury on Sea

Burgh Island
Tel: 01548-810 514;
www.burghisland.com.
Unusual Art Deco hotel on an island first inhabited in AD900 by monks, with access by sea tractor. Agatha Christie wrote two books while staying here. The smart clientele dress up for dinner dances. *£££*

Combe Martin

Sandy Cove Hotel
Old Coast Road; tel: 01271-882 243;
www.sandycove-hotel.co.uk.
Expect unpretentious style and warmth at this family hotel with a spectacular outlook over the bay. The swimming pool has a sliding glass roof *££*

Dartmouth

Royal Castle Hotel

The Quay; tel: 01803-833 033; www.royalcastle.co.uk.

This former 17th-century coaching inn on the quay is a focus of the town's social scene, with lively bars, great ambience and a respected restaurant. ££

Plymouth

Duke of Cornwall

Millbay Road; tel: 01752-275 850; www.thedukeofcornwall.co.uk.

A true Plymouth landmark, Victorian Gothic architecture sets the tone for the character that follows inside. A stone's throw from the historic Hoe, this represents very pleasant, value-for-money accommodation. ££

Princetown

Plume of Feathers

Tel: 01822-890 240; www.plumeoffeathersdartmoor.co.uk.

The oldest building (1795) on the high moor, this traditional inn has original features, lots of character and warm hospitality. Accommodation ranges from bunk house to en suite. £

Ilfracombe

The Elmfield Hotel

Torrs Park; tel: 01271-863 377; www.theelmfield.com; bus stop 5 mins' walk from hotel near Tunnels Beaches.

A family-friendly independent hotel housed in a restored Victorian villa. There's plenty to do: indoor swimming pool, family workshops, games facilities, cine screen, or just chill-out in the lovely gardens. ££

The Hamptons Hotel

Torrs Park; tel: 01271-864 246; www.thehamptonshotel.com; bus stop 5 mins' walk from hotel near Tunnels Beaches.

Every room is in a different style at this chic boutique hotel just below the NT Coastal Path. Outstanding made-to-order breakfasts such as Eggs Benedict served in the stylish restaurant. ££

Bolventor

Jamaica Inn

Nr Launceston; tel: 01566-86250; www.jamaicainn.co.uk.

The famous inn in a dramatic setting on the Bodmin Moor has recently expanded but retains its snug, cosy atmosphere – and its ghost. It also boasts a Smugglers Museum. ££

Fowey

Old Quay House Hotel

28 Fore Street; tel: 01726-833 302; www.theoldquayhouse.com.

A lovingly restored boutique hotel in an old building. The terrace is the perfect place for pre-dinner drinks and to soak up the estuary atmosphere. £££

Newquay

Headland Hotel

Tel: 01637-872 211; www.headlandhotel.co.uk.

Grand, imposing appearance but with a family-friendly atmosphere. The hotel has an indoor swimming pool and spa and is set in 10 acres (4 hectares) above Fistral Beach. £££

Penzance

Abbey Hotel

Abbey Street; tel: 01736-366 906; www.theabbeyonline.co.uk; near main bus and rail stations.

Delightful sky-blue 17th-century building overlooking the harbour with a gentlemen's club atmosphere. Rooms are tastefully furnished and there is an excellent oak-panelled restaurant and a pretty walled garden. ££–£££

St Austell

Carlyon Bay Hotel

Sea Road; tel: 01726-812 304; www.brend-hotels.co.uk/thecarlyonbay.

Luxurious 1930s hotel set in 250 acres (100 hectares) of expansive subtropical gardens, with leisure facilities including golf. £££

St Ives

Garrack Hotel

Burthallan Lane; tel: 01736-796 199; www.garrack.com.

Set on a hill near the Tate, this family-run hotel has a large garden offering great views over Porthmeor Beach. There's an indoor spa pool, a sauna and an award-winning restaurant. Private on-site parking is available. ££

Primrose Valley Hotel

Primrose Valley; tel: 01736-794 939; www.primroseonline.co.uk.

Winner of several green awards, this chic, relaxed Edwardian villa has Forest Stewardship Council approved wooden floors, natural soap, strict recycling and energy-saving policies. It is fun too! ££

Tintagel

Bossiney House Hotel

Tel: 01840-770 240; www.bossineyhouse.com.

In a great location far from the madding crowd (0.5 miles/1km from the village) and with superb views, heated indoor pool and a respected restaurant. £

Isles of Scilly

The Harbourside Hotel

St Mary's; tel: 01720-422 352; www.harboursidescilly.co.uk.

On the quay, near sandy beaches and a stone's throw away from where boats depart for the other islands. Fishing, bike hire, golf; taxi service to/from heliport. £

USEFUL WEBSITES

www.visitdevon.co.uk
www.visitcornwall.com
www.nationaltrust.org.uk
www.westcountrycottages.co.uk
www.helpfulholidays.com
www.coastandcountry.co.uk
www.toadhallcottages.co.uk
www.forestholidays.co.uk
www.luxique.com
www.laterooms.com
www.cornishfarmholidays.co.uk
www.yha.org.uk
www.devonholidays.org
www.organicholidays.co.uk
www.cornishtipiholidays.co.uk
www.smoothhound.co.uk

Below: Tintagel is a beautiful place to stay.

Index

Credits

Insight Great Breaks Devon and Cornwall
Written by: Andrew Eames, Roland Collins, Pam Barrett, Roger Williams and Veronica Garbutt
Updated by: Hilary Weston and Jackie Staddon
Edited by: Siân Lezard and Alexia Georgiou
Art Editor: Richard Cooke
Maps: APA Publications
Publishing Manager: Rachel Fox
Series Editor: Carine Tracanelli

All pictures by Lydia Evans/APA except: Alamy 109; Stuart Berry 55C; Aaron Bihari 31B; David Bleasdale 95B; Carlyon Bay Hotel 124; Tim Brown 59T; Fotolia 74B, 75B, 102, 108; Fotolibra 5BL, 59B; Tim Hall 119; Hoxtonboy 30T; Max Hughes 105B; Istockphoto 4BL, 15, 20B, 21B, 24B, 32B, 34T, 49T, 58B, 60B, 62T, 74T, 91R, 93B, 96T, 115, 122; Rachel Lambert 87B; NTPL 83B, 118; Occombe Fram 26T; Tom Page 97B; Danny Pyne 82; Rex Features 36C; Ronald Grant 36/37; Scilly Isles TB 110/111, 110B, 117T; Tom Smyth/APA 4TL, 38, 39, 40, 41, 46, 48T&B, 49B, 50T&B, 51T, 52T&B, 55T, 56B, 60/61, 61B, 115C, 116, 120B, 121, 123; UK Country House Hotels 53; Matt Wharton 84T; Tamsyn Williams 78/79; Corrie Wingate/APA 54, 62B, 63T; Scott Zona 70T.

Cover pictures by: (front) Spila Riccardo/SIME (T), istockphoto (BL, BR); (back) APA/Lydia Evans.

CONTACTING THE EDITORS: As every effort is made to provide accurate information in this publication, we would appreciate it if readers would call our attention to any errors and omissions by contacting:
Apa Publications, PO Box 7910, London SE1 1WE, England.
insight@apaguide.co.uk

Information has been obtained from sources believed to be reliable, but its accuracy and completeness, and the opinions based thereon, are not guaranteed.

Second Edition 2013

Printed by CTPS - China

Worldwide distribution enquiries:
APA Publications GmbH & Co. Verlag KG (Singapore Branch)
7030 Ang Mo Kio Ave 5,
08-65 Northstar @ AMK, Singapore 569880
apasin@singnet.com.sg

Distributed in the UK and Ireland by:
Dorling Kindersley Ltd
A Penguin Group company
80 Strand, London, WC2R 0RL, UK
customerservice@dk.com